THE REFERENDUM

JO GRIMOND
&
BRIAN NEVE

Rex Collings • London • 1975

First published by Rex Collings Ltd
69 Marylebone High Street London W 1

SBN Paperback 90172086 0
~~Hardback   90172091 7~~

Typeset by Malvern Typesetting Services and
printed in Great Britain
at the University Printing House, Cambridge
(Euan Phillips, University Printer)

Contents

Preface

This book does not deal with any events later than 1 May 1975.

We should like to thank Mr Trevor Smith for his most valuable assistance and advice during the writing of this book.

In addition we would like to thank Catherine Fisher and Jackie Lebe for their typing and Mr Dave Lewis for assistance in gathering research material.

We would also like to thank Social Surveys (Gallup Poll) Ltd and NOP Market Research Limited for permission to republish copyright material.

1   The Political Context of the Common Market Referendum

Why is Britain about to hold its first national referendum? Why have the normal processes of party and parliamentary government been set aside in the hope of finally deciding the question of Britain's membership of the Common Market? In this chapter, in attempting to answer these questions, we first summarize the political history of the Common Market issue in the 1960s and then trace the emergence of the idea of a referendum on the question in the early 1970s.

1   The Liberal Party
The Liberal Party is the only Party which from the outset maintained that Britain should have signed the Treaty of Rome and joined in the Coal and Steel Communities and the Common Market. Although there has always been a minority in the Party which was against joining the EEC, the majority has been wholly consistent in its views from the outset. Jo Grimond long stressed the need for Scottish representation in Brussels.

2   SNP and Plaid Cymru
The official policy of both parties has been opposed to joining the EEC. The SNP oppose entry because Scotland will neither have any separate say in the decision nor any representation in Brussels.

3   Conservative Government and Labour Opposition 1960-1964
Conservative Government: The Conservative Party has

traditionally given its leader great authority, especially when he is Prime Minister. For so long as a Conservative Prime Minister is successful he is rarely challenged from within his party. The leader's freedom of action is increased by the party's general antipathy to high ideology or to very elaborate programmes of policy.

Thus Harold Macmillan was able in 1960 to begin to win over his Cabinet and party to the idea of an attempt to join the Common Market. By the Common Market we refer principally to the European Economic Community, but also to the European Coal and Steel Community and Euratom (The European Atomic Energy Community).* In 1959 Britain had joined with six other countries in forming the European Free Trade Association (EFTA). Britain had refused to join the EEC at its inception in 1957 and prior to 1960 the Cabinet and the Civil Service had generally been against British membership. In that year, however, Macmillan became aware of several pressures in favour of British entry.

It is likely that Macmillan's main motives were political: that he saw Britain regaining a major world role within a united Europe. In 1960 an Economic Steering Committee of senior civil servants under Sir Fred Lee, Permanent Secretary to the Treasury, recommended an attempt at entry mainly for political reasons. The economic arguments were felt to be balanced. Macmillan, following Churchill, had a rather grand conception of British foreign policy in relation to the three circles of America, the Commonwealth, and Europe. His policy of promoting detente had suffered as a result of the U-2 incident and the collapse of the Paris summit of May 1962. Further, the Americans indicated in 1960 that they

---

* The institution of the three bodies joined in 1967 as a result of the 'merger Treaty' of 1965. The official title was thereafter the 'European Communities'.

took the EEC more seriously than EFTA—the trading bloc of which Britain was a member.

Macmillan knew that the objections to Britain's joining would centre around the Commonwealth, agriculture, and sovereignty and that on all three issues there was traditionally strong Conservative feeling. Thus from the end of 1960 when he had come round to the view that Britain ought to apply to join the EEC, Macmillan was extremely cautious in moving towards a formal application. However, so successful was he in selling the European idea to his party that, in July 1961, when the Prime Minister announced the British intention to begin negotiations, only 20 Conservative MPs abstained on the resolution in the House approving the initiative. The Labour Party abstained on the vote.

In October Edward Heath, who was responsible for the negotiations, said that Britain accepted the Treaty of Rome and the political consequences but sought specific safeguards on agriculture. The negotiations in late 1961 and 1962 were complex and detailed. The issues were presented as primarily economic rather than political. After dealing with the Commonwealth, negotiations centred on agriculture and by October 1962 deadlock had been reached. By this time the Labour Party had altered its position (as we shall see in the next section) and Macmillan's position within his Cabinet had been weakened by the 'night of the long knives' of 13 July 1962 and the declining electoral prospects for the Conservatives. In late July 40 MPs had signed a motion urging the Government to stand firm in the agricultural negotiations. In November 1962 there were signs of a division of opinion in the Cabinet with Iain Macleod stressing that Britain must not pay too high a price for membership and other Ministers also indicated that Britain would survive without the EEC.

Macmillan, however, had retained control of his

Cabinet on the issue. But in January 1963 President de Gaulle effectively vetoed the question of British membership by arguing that the English were not ready for membership. His reasons may have been influenced by the position taken by the British in the negotiations or his increased suspicion of the British-American relationship in the light of the Polaris agreement of December 1961.

Labour Opposition: The issue of British membership of the Common Market is a complex and unique one in modern British politics, in part because the implications of membership for Britain are speculative. Further, the issue cannot easily be categorized or placed into the conventional left-right framework of British politics. An opinion on the question involves a complex series of judgements—on the nature of the EEC and on what it is likely to become, and on how one perceives the future of Britain as a nation state.

This difficulty in defining the nature of the issue has played havoc with the Labour Party—traditionally highly concerned with policy compared to the Tories. In the early 1960s most Gaitskellites supported British membership while the Left was generally opposed. Labour policy, however, was generally favourable to entry from 1960 to mid-1962. The Labour Party abstained on the vote on the beginning of negotiations in August 1961 and in June 1962 all three party leaders agreed that the best solution was entry to the EEC on good terms.

Gaitskell had fought and fought to reverse the 1960 Party Conference decision in favour of unilateral nuclear disarmament. This he did at the 1961 Conference, so arousing the suspicion of the Left. On Europe, however, to the great annoyance and surprise of pro-Europeans like George Brown, Gaitskell made a speech at the 1962 Party Conference which was distinctly hostile to the EEC. He was cheered by the Left and much of the unity of the

4

Party, shattered in 1960–61, was restored.

Had de Gaulle not vetoed the British approach, the Common Market might have become a central issue in the General Election (something that it has never been). Under Gaitskell's leadership the Party would probably have taken a generally anti-Market stance but (and this problem was to remain with the Party) they would have had to have made concessions in their electoral stance to the pro-Market wing of the party.

At the Conference Gaitskell formally spoke to present the National Executive Committee statement. This stipulated five conditions which would be required for joining the EEC. The main conditions were 'strong and binding safeguards' for the Commonwealth, freedom to pursue an independent foreign policy and to plan 'our own economy', fulfillment of the pledge made to associates in EFTA and guarantees for British agriculture. Gaitskell argued that those who wanted British membership should provide proof that it would help solve Britain's problems. He went on:

> When Mr Macmillan speaks of belonging to a larger political unit what does he mean by 'belonging'? What are we supposed to be joining?

He admitted that federation might never come but pointed out the implications of federation if it did come: 'This is what it means; it does mean the end of Britain as an independent nation state.' He also talked, in this context, of the end of a thousand years of history. Emotionally, the speech was anti-Market and George Brown had rather desperately to keep the pro-Market voice alive when he summed up in the debate. The TGWU, who were to be consistent opponents of EEC entry, paid for Gaitskell's speech to be widely distributed in the Party. The Conference resulted in an uneasy compromise and a division of opinion in the Labour Party which was to haunt it in future years.

5

4 The Labour Government and Europe 1964-1970

Given de Gaulle's veto the Common Market ceased to be a live issue for some years. Wilson had been a prominent anti-Marketeer in Opposition and was felt to be even less favourable to the EEC than Gaitskell. The Common Market was hardly a topic in the 1964 Election or in the subsequent two years. The 1964 Labour manifesto expressed pride in the Commonwealth and argued that the Conservatives were willing to sacrifice it to the interests of the Common Market.

Although the leadership kept to Gaitskell's five conditions, George Brown's prominence as First Secretary in the Cabinet gave hope to pro-Marketeers of a more sympathetic attitude to membership. Whereas the 1966 Labour manifesto was guarded, the Conservatives at this time, under their new leader, Edward Heath, were now strongly committed to Europe. Heath even said that he was prepared to accept the Common Agricultural Policy.

It has been suggested that Harold Wilson wanted to 'do something else' following the economic crisis of July 1966, after which planning for growth was abandoned and a deflationary policy adopted to support sterling. Aware of the opposition within his Cabinet and his party, Wilson controlled the decision-making process carefully and in a way similar to that of Macmillan in the early 1960s. The decision to go ahead with European talks was a narrow one. On 10 November 1966 the Prime Minister announced that the Government had decided 'that a new high level approach must now be made to see whether the conditions exist—or do not exist—for fruitful negotiation and the basis on which such negotiations could take place'. He added: 'We mean business'. In order to try and carry the doubters in his Cabinet Wilson was to accompany George Brown, his Foreign Secretary, in the series of pre-negotiation talks in various European capitals. These talks were held between January and

6

March 1967. George Brown reports in his autobiography that the Prime Minister took a surprisingly firm line in favour of Britain's applying to join the Market.

While the talks took place there were signs of opposition to the Prime Minister's considered strategy of building a Cabinet majority in favour of making an application. In February 1967, 108 Labour MPs signed a motion against precipitate entry without safeguards for British and Commonwealth interests. The same month Douglas Jay, the President of the Board of Trade, had made a strong speech hostile to the EEC at a private meeting of Labour MPs.

In May 1967 estimates put the number of unconditional opponents of membership in the Cabinet at 6 but by then a momentum had gathered and Wilson himself was committed to making a formal application for entry. (It would have been difficult for the Cabinet to decide against making an application at that stage without doing damage to the image of the Prime Minister and thus to the Party's own electoral prospects.)

Anti-Market ministers knew, however (as did Labour backbenchers of a similar mind) that the French attitudes made the chances of the negotiations being successful rather doubtful. Wilson had reported to the Cabinet as early as February 1967 that a French veto was likely and this was the view of officials at the British Embassy in Paris. This may well have been crucial in explaining the unanimous acceptance by the Cabinet of Wilson's policy as well as its support at the October Party Conference.

On 10 May 1967 the application was approved by the House of Commons by 488 votes to 62. 35 Labour MPs voted against the Government and 50 others abstained. Only a few days later, however, at a press conference on 16 May President de Gaulle talked of the obstacles to British entry and urged delay until Britain had carried through a fundamental economic and political transformation. Wilson said he would not take no for an answer and his position was supported at the Party Conference. The application was already doomed, however, and on 27 November President de Gaulle, for the second time, finally and categorically vetoed the opening of negotiations.

In June 1969 General de Gaulle was succeeded as French President by Georges Pompidou. At the Party Conference in October George Brown argued that the Government's application remained on the table and that he was waiting to see whether our continental European colleagues would agree that negotiations should begin. An NEC statement indicating the Government's view was accepted but the Conference also accepted a hostile TGWU resolution stressing the safeguards needed against any interference with national, internal policy making. In December, at an EEC summit meeting at the Hague, the member countries agreed to re-open negotiations with Britain in the near future.

Fulfilling a pledge made at the 1969 Party Conference the Government issued a White Paper on the costs of EEC entry in February 1970. Negotiations for entry were to start in the summer. In January 1970 the Prime Minister said that the Government wished to confine the negotiations to the 'few important questions which had to be resolved before it could take the decision to join the community'. Minor questions, he said, could be solved within the Community. On 10 February he told the House that 'Government and Parliament can take their decisions in full confidence that on fair terms we can stand and profit by the far more competitive situation that entry into the Market implies.' The Government, he added 'will enter into negotiations resolutely with good faith . . .'.

How Labour Government negotiations with the EEC countries would have fared no one will know: the General Election of June 1970 returned the Conservatives to power. It is the opinion of the author of the major work on the politics of the Common Market issue up to 1972 that had the Labour Government negotiated with the EEC in the summer of 1970 this would very probably have led to British membership. A number of members of the Labour Cabinet of 1970 later said that the terms achieved by the Conservative Government would have been acceptable to a Labour Cabinet.

Certainly it seems that, as in 1967, the Prime Minister and the majority of his Cabinet had in 1970 committed themselves so firmly to the idea of entry that they would have fought strongly for a pro-Market position (if necessary enforcing Cabinet responsibility and forcing dissidents to abide by the majority opinion or else resign). The imponderable is the extent of the anti-Market revolt. Well aware of the lessons of Ramsay MacDonald in 1932 Harold Wilson would not have wanted to enter the EEC on a vote with more Conservatives than Labour votes in favour, though he may have had little choice in the matter. In April 1975 the majority of Labour MPs voted against the re-negotiated terms Wilson had secured at the Dublin summit as a basis for Britain staying in the EEC. Whatever would have happened if the Labour Government had remained in power or won the Election, out of office the distribution of power was changed in a way that was bound to influence the Party's attitude to the European question and lead to a different set of tactical considerations.

5 Conservative Government and Labour Opposition 1970–1971
In the campaign of 1970 all the leaders of the three major parties took a somewhat similar line—a line which has been summed up as 'We must look at the terms but we should go in if the terms are right'. The Liberals however were adamant in their commitment to the European idea

9

and stressed that they continued to believe that the necessary amendments to the Common Market policies e.g. the CAP could be negotiated from within. The SNP, Plaid Cymru and the majority of Ulster Unionists were opposed to entry. The Labour manifesto pledged a Labour Government to press the negotiations with determination, 'with the purpose of joining the enlarged community provided that British and essential Commonwealth interests can be safeguarded'. The Conservatives were strongly committed to British membership: Edward Heath said on 5 May however:

> It would not be in the interest of the Community that enlargement should take place except with the full-hearted consent of the Parliaments and peoples of the new Member countries.

Both leaders specifically rejected the idea of a referendum on the issue. The Conservative Government 'picked up' the Labour application and began negotiations on 30 June, only two weeks after the election. Detailed negotiations began in 1970 and ran through to February 1971.

The prospects for significant revolt within the Conservative Government and party were poor. Only about 20 Conservative MPs had voted against the Government's proposal to apply for membership in 1967. The anti-Market Conservatives were generally rather distant from Edward Heath and few were in the Government. Not only were the numbers small, but there were few channels through which to mobilize and make such opposition effective in the Conservative Party, especially when the Party is in government. The National Union in the Conservative Party has no power comparable to the National Executive Committee in the Labour Party and the Tory Central Office unlike Transport House is under the control of a nominee of the leader. In the particular circumstances of 1970 the opportunities for dissent were even fewer. Edward Heath as leader and Prime Minister, was a dominating man 'amongst his peers' and in his party and also a man totally committed to getting Britain into the Common Market; moreover he had won the Election almost single-handed and against the predictions of opinion polls and 'informed comment'.

Conservative opponents of the Common Market had been among the first to support the idea of a referendum on the issue. 38 Conservatives, including Robin Turton, Henry Legge-Bourke and Derek Walker-Smith, supported a ten-minute Bill introduced in December 1969 by Bruce Campbell (Cons. Oldham West). The Bill provided for a referendum on Britain's entry into the Market.

As will be seen in the next chapter, power is much less centralized in the Labour Party and dissent can more easily be mobilized. At the 1969 Party Conference the latent anti-Market feeling in the Party had come nearer to the surface. Further, Hugh Scanlon had become leader of the AEUW in 1969 and was likely to join with Jack Jones of the TGWU in the latter's long standing hostility to the EEC. At the 1970 Conference the NEC statement was carried by a large majority. This statement, similar to previous NEC statements since 1967, was as follows:

> This Conference is of the opinion that negotiations should continue with the EEC to see whether entry can be achieved on acceptable terms and so that the real costs and benefits may be assessed.
>
> Entry to the Common Market should depend on proper safeguards being secured in relation to the share of Community finance to be borne by the UK, restructuring of the Common Agricultural Programme and protection for Commonwealth and EFTA interests.

Following the 1970 Election Douglas Jay had put forward the idea of a referendum on the Common Market in an article in the *Times*. As a Gaitskellite, however, Jay was not likely to attract much support. On 4 November 1970 Jay was joined by Anthony Wedgwood Benn who argued (in a letter to his constituents) that because of the transfer of sovereignty implicit in membership of the European Community some 'unique mechanism' was needed to consult the people on the question. Benn's support for a Common Market referendum was linked to his general argument for more decentralization and participation in British politics. He argued that there were such sharp differences of opinion within each party that a general election could not decide the issue. He had originally opposed the Market, then supported British membership from 1967 on; in 1970 he seemed to be reconsidering his position again. In December 1970 a proposal by the TGWU for a referendum was defeated in the National Executive Committee. Instead the NEC decided to hold a special Party Conference on the Common Market 'before Parliament decided the issue'.

Opinion began to polarize within the Party.* In the last ten days of January 1971, 119 Labour MPs signed an early day motion that 'entry to the Common Market on the terms so far envisaged would be against the interests of the country.' In May 1971, 100 Labour MPs signed a pro-Market advertisement, published by the Labour Committee for Europe, in the *Guardian*. There was considerable talk in early 1971 that if Harold Wilson was unwilling to lead Labour against the Market, another leader would. That potential leader was James Callaghan. At a press lunch on 17 February Callaghan said in effect that it was the Opposition's job to oppose. He said that 'Heath must be able to rely on a majority of the Commons from his own party'. Further, Wilson could no longer rely

---

* The subsequent account in this section draws on Uwe Kitzinger's *Diplomacy and Persuasion*.

12

on a majority in the NEC for British entry. Benn was now voting anti-Market. As Kitzinger argues, if Wilson stuck to his pro-Market position there would be a party split with a ready-made alternative leader 'as well as a large part of the Parliamentary Party, the Unions, the Conference, and the rank and file against him.' Another factor which strengthened the pressures on the Labour Party to change its position on the Common Market was the low support for entry indicated by public opinion polls. Opinion polls conducted by NOP Market Research Limited in March and October 1970 and March 1971 found only 22, 24 and 27% approval respectively for Britain joining the Common Market. On average, (in the three polls) 64% disapproved of entry.

It was not certain that the Government's negotiations would be successful and Wilson reserved his position. He was active in making sure that the special Party Conference in July was merely a consultative one. In his summing-up speech in July he recognized the gathering strength in his Party of the anti-Marketeers by indicating that he felt some of the terms to be unacceptable. He also argued that pressure alone would not deflect him from his duty as leader of the Party to recommend the course he believed to be right. He continued:

> Nor from my duty—and I have always regarded this as the duty of the Leader—to do all in my power to maintain the unity of this Party.

To have supported Heath's terms might well have severely split the Party. It might also have lost him the leadership.

After the special conference the NEC passed by 16-6 on 28 July 1971 a resolution which rejected entry on the terms negotiated by the Conservative Government and called on the Prime Minister to submit to the democratic judgement of a general election: it also called on the Parliamentary Labour Party to unite wholeheartedly in

13

voting against the Government's policy. This was the crucial decision. It became the NEC statement at the Party Conference in October and was there adopted as Party policy by an overwhelming 5:1 ratio.

At the Conference a resolution calling on the Party to press for the withdrawal of Britain's application to the EEC was defeated. More significantly the Post Office Engineering Union supported the NEC statement but proposed an amendment which would provide for a referendum before a final decision was taken, if there were no General Election before entry. The amendment was defeated by 1,928,000 votes to 4,161,000 but it was an early and explicit manifestation of the argument that if the decision were left to Parliament, no matter which party was in government, there would be a parliamentary majority for British membership.

The conference policy was accepted by the leadership. Harold Wilson's closing speech to the Conference was interpreted by some observers as giving Labour Marketeers the go-ahead to vote against their Party on the vote on 28 October on British entry into the EEC. In practice he was probably recognizing the inevitable. In the House of Commons vote (on the principle of entry into the EEC) there were 356 votes in favour to 244 votes against, with 22 abstentions. Despite a three-line whip, 69 Labour MPs voted with the Government. 39 Conservatives and Ulster Unionist MPs voted with the Opposition.

6 The Referendum Idea 1972-1975

i *Introduction:* A party in Opposition must both oppose the Government and collectively rethink its own philosophy, or its policy, or both. The Labour Party had declared itself to be against entry on the Conservative terms and following the first reading the pressure on the pro-Market Labour MPs to toe the Party line—of 'all-out and straight opposition'—was strengthened. Many in the Party felt that the Government could be defeated on their European Communities Bill but only if the pro-Market MPs, led symbolically if not formally by Roy Jenkins, voted against the Government.

Much of the feeling generated by the party division reflected the traditional split in the Party between left and right. Many in the Party felt that the leadership had become remote from the rank and file and the Left, especially, wished to ensure that Party Conference decisions were adhered to by the Parliamentary Party and the Shadow Cabinet. Thus the pressure was put on the pro-Marketeers.

In early 1972 there was still little desire in the Labour Party for a referendum. But the cause had been greatly advanced by the decision at the 1971 Conference to elect Anthony Wedgwood Benn as Party Chairman for the year 1971-72. The Chairman presides over the National Executive Committee, the body responsible under the Party Constitution for party policy when the Party Conference is not in session. We have seen that in 1970 he had discussed favourably the idea of a referendum on the Common Market issue. In November 1971 he spoke of the danger of the public losing faith in the political system if they came to believe that 'the limited democratic choice open to them only once in five years could be frustrated by temporary alliances across the floor to carry through constitutional changes that had never been tested politically at the polls'. During 1972 the Labour Party was making policy at two levels and in both the Party Chairman was in a strong position of influence. The first was the day-to-day policy of conducting the parliamentary opposition to the European Communities Bill. The second was the work by a number of party committees, representing all sections of the Party, in preparing a consultative policy document which would be submitted to the 1972 Conference and which would form the basis of a manifesto if a snap election were called. Some of these committees began work soon after the Election defeat. The object of one of these committees, which was established early in 1972, was to work out a party policy on the Common Market which could be included in any manifesto. There were reports in early March that the drafters of the policy programme were considering the idea of a promise that a Labour Government would consult the people on any new EEC Bill, possibly by a referendum.

ii *Referendum Amendment February-April 1972:* We shall return to this process of policy drafting but the immediate issue in 1972, and the issue on which the idea of a referendum first became prominent, was the tactical policy adopted by the Labour Party on the Government's European Communities Bill. The Bill received its second reading in February 1972 by 309 votes to 301, a majority of 8. Edward Heath had been forced to make the vote a matter of confidence. Conservatives have argued that the Bill would have been defeated if the Government had not made it a 'confidence' vote,* while some observers reported that had the Government's majority been in danger Roy Jenkins and several other Labour pro-marketeers would have supported the Bill.

The narrow vote greatly encouraged those who felt that the Government would be defeated on the Bill, which faced a protracted committee stage. One of the amendments on the Commons Order Paper for the committee stage was tabled by anti-Market Tories calling for a referendum before Britain entered the EEC. The

---

* Neil Marten, a Tory anti-marketeer has said precisely this. *Times,* 1 April 1975. By 'confidence' vote we mean, that the Prime Minister had made it clear that, if the Government were defeated, he would ask the Queen for a dissolution of Parliament (i.e. call for a General Election).

principal sponsors of the motion were Neil Marten, Derek Walker-Smith, Robin Turton, and Anthony Fell. All were senior Tories; all had voted against the Bill on the second reading. The amendment provided that no date for British entry be set until a consultative advisory referendum had been held, thus enabling the Government to assess the extent to which the Treaty of Accession had the full-hearted consent of the British people. There was no Labour amendment down to this effect. The only comparable Opposition amendment, in the names of Michael Foot, Peter Shore, and Fred Peart, provided for a General Election before entry. This reflected the Party's policy as decided at the Party Conference of October 1971.

On Wednesday, 15 March 1972 the Shadow Cabinet met for its weekly meeting. At the meeting it was decided that the Party should not support the Tory amendment. The grounds for this decision were that the last Party Conference had defeated a resolution calling for a referendum. There were apparently only four votes in favour, one of them coming from Benn. Harold Wilson voted against. The next day, the 16th, President Pompidou of France announced that a referendum would be held in France to ratify the entry of Britain and the other candidate countries into the Common Market. That evening Benn said that there must be a nation-wide campaign for a General Election or a referendum in Britain on the issue. He told a meeting of the Parliamentary Labour Party on the 16th that he would press the NEC (of which he was Chairman) to reconsider the Conference decision against a referendum. This seemed to be part of a strategy to get the PLP and the Parliamentary Committee (Shadow Cabinet) to make his proposal Party policy.

The announcement of the French referendum thus had a considerable impact. Benn spoke on the 17th (at a

17

meeting of the Christian Socialist Movement) in favour of referenda. At the next meeting of the National Executive Committee on 22 March, a resolution from Benn inviting the PLP to reconsider the idea of a referendum was passed by 13 votes to 11. Benn argued that in the circumstances a referendum might be the only practicable means of meeting the spirit of the Party Conference decision. The pro-Marketeers voted against the resolution. This was an important vote: the NEC had shifted the mass Party's official position on the referendum idea. The Shadow Cabinet decided to consider the NEC resolution the next week.

On 24 March 1972 Direct Rule was imposed on Northern Ireland. Part of the package announced was a provision for a system of regular plebiscites in Northern Ireland about the border. The first was to be held 'as soon as practicable in the near future', Heath announced in the House of Commons. Benn used this innovation as a further argument for having a referendum on EEC entry. In another speech Benn urged that the Common Market issue must be settled in 1972 by a General Election or referendum.

Finally, on 29 March 1972 the Shadow Cabinet decided by 8 votes to 6 to reverse its previous position and to recommend Labour support for the Conservative referendum amendment. Wilson and Short changed their votes. It was decided that this recommendation should be made to a meeting of the PLP. If accepted, there would be a Labour whip in favour of the Tory Amendment. Clearly the *volte face* owed much to the work of Tony Benn as Party Chairman; later justifying the move Harold Wilson referred to the French referendum, the Northern Ireland plebiscite decision and the NEC decision as crucial factors in influencing some Shadow Cabinet members to change their minds.

However tactical the decision, for the first time both

18

wings of the Party were in favour of the idea of a referendum and Wilson himself—long on record as opposed to referenda—had voted for support of the Conservative amendment. What he almost certainly did not calculate (or fully understand) was the pressure this would put on the pro-Marketeers in the Shadow Cabinet. For if the European Communities Bill were to be threatened the question was whether Jenkins and the Labour Marketeers would save the Government and so expose themselves to the hostility of the Left.

The split came on 10 April 1972 the first day back after the Easter recess. Roy Jenkins resigned as Deputy Leader of the Party and George Thomson and Harold Lever resigned their Shadow Cabinet posts. In his letter to Harold Wilson Roy Jenkins gave several reasons for his resignation. Firstly he felt that 'the official majority position of the Party, which was one of opposition to the terms of entry to the EEC, has increasingly become one of opposition in principle'. He cited specifically the Shadow Cabinet decision on 29 March; to Jenkins it was wrong in itself and was taken without a 'full appraisal of the possible consequences'. He speculated on the damage to the Labour Party of a referendum campaign on which the Party was divided and also condemned the referendum in principle as a device liable to undermine parliamentary responsibility. He argued that it would make consistancy in government more difficult, that its use could not be limited, once introduced, and that it could be a 'powerful continuing weapon against progressive legislation'. Finally, he argued that the announcement of the French referendum had 'increased the temptation to exploit the issue for short term political advantage'. This is not the way, he argued, in which an Opposition should be run. 'If Government is born out of opportunism', he added, 'it becomes not merely difficult but impossible'.

Thus the first impact of the referendum proposal,

generally seen as a compromise between different sections of the Party, was to increase dissension. The other effect was to make the passage of the Bill considerably safer for the Conservative Government. On 12 April the PLP voted 129-96 in favour of the Shadow Cabinet recommendation that the Opposition support the Tory amendment. On 18 April 1972 the amendment was easily defeated in the House of Commons by 284 votes to 235. Jenkins, Lever, Thomson and others felt freer to defy the two-line Labour whip and abstain and this put the result beyond question.

The position of both the Party and the Party leadership had changed and although Wilson referred to a referendum as a 'very poor second best' and as 'pretty repugnant' he argued that it was necessary in order that—in the absence of a General Election—the country be consulted on a 'major constitutional change'. The argument that entry into the EEC was a 'major constitutional change', had not been heard in the 1960s, but constitutional changes have in many countries been traditionally referred to referenda and the association of ideas added legitimacy to the proposal. It was known at this time that Eire, Norway and Denmark were to hold referenda on EEC membership before the end of 1972.

Although it led to a significant change of stance the whole approach of the Labour Party in relation to the Marten amendment had been largely tactical and it was not clear that the referendum commitment would be part of the Party's longer term policy. The position of Benn (the party Chairman) was clear, but Wilson's was not. Benn argued during the debate on the referendum amendment that if there were an election he felt the Party should include provision for a referendum in its manifesto. He claimed that this would be the only way to put the issue to the public.

The result of the episode of the Marten amendment was to indicate to Wilson that a Party position against the

Market in principle would split the Party. Jenkins and the pro-Marketeers could not unite at an Election on such a platform. Wilson was aware that the Tribune Group was hoping to get a commitment by the Party to withdraw from the EEC if they formed the next Government. The 1971 Conference had demanded a General Election before entry. Yet the Party clearly would not unite at such an Election. Thus, assuming Britain was a member of the EEC when any new Labour Government came to power, there would be a commitment to renegotiation. That, however, might merely delay the clash. Further, with a Conservative Opposition, the Left would fear that the pressures to remain a member would be strong. The idea of a referendum began to seem to be of more than short term tactical advantage to the Party. However, nothing was yet decided concerning the Party's stand on the Common Market in the consultative document being produced for the 1972 Party Conference and as a possible draft manifesto for any Election held in late 1972 or early 1973.

The majority of the Liberal Party MPs on the whole were against a referendum, though some including David Steel and Jo Grimond had voted for it. The SNP and Plaid Cymru favoured it.

iii *Labour's Common Market Strategy; 1972 and after:* In a speech in June Wilson stressed that the Party's policy was opposition to the terms negotiated for entry to the EEC, not to the principle of entry itself. He tried to identify a consistent policy of approval if the terms were right—tracing back to the NEC statements of 1962. (In this he rather glossed over the much more enthusiastic political acceptance of the Market which seemed to be his Government's policy in 1969.) Wilson went on to comment on the discussions in the NEC on the Party document:

I have said to the National Executive Committee of the Labour Party that in my view in these circumstances the people should have the right to decide the issue of principle involved, when the outcome of negotiations is clear—and to decide it by a national free vote, a national referendum, on this issue and this issue only.

At the same time the Tribune group was demanding renegotiations but on terms so strong that it would be difficult to envisage the Community accepting them. The conditions strongly indicating their priorities included the following:

a abandonment of the Common Agricultural Policy and of Value Added Tax;

b no limitations on the freedom of a Labour Government to carry out regional plans and the extension of public ownership;

c no restriction on the Labour Government's power to control movements of capital into and out of the UK; and

d the preservation of the power of the UK Parliament over its legislation, taxation and regulations.

On the proposal for a referendum or a General Election, on the results of a successful renegotiation, there seemed to be agreement. At the NEC meeting to discuss the final draft document all but two members accepted a statement which committed a Labour Government to negotiate the terms of entry on a number of specific points, including agricultural policy and the sovereignty of Parliament. If the negotiations were successful the new terms would be put to the electorate through a referendum or General Election. Another clause provided that if the negotiations were unsuccessful the British people be consulted on the advisability of withdrawal from the Community. This last clause suggests the

22

possible scenario favoured by the Left, of a General Election on the issue of withdrawal. This, however, would have entailed a divided Party. There seems no doubt that Wilson—as he implied in June—was banking on successful negotiations followed by a referendum.

Thus on 26 July 1972, the consultative document was published as 'Labour's Programme for Britain'. The statement included the following points.

a opposition to the Common Market on the terms negotiated by the Conservative Government;

b renegotiation;

c a General Election or referendum if the renegotiations are successful; and

d consultation of the British people if the renegotiations do not succeed.

This consultative document provided the basis for the NEC statement on the EEC put before the Party Conference. Also to be voted on at the Conference were two other resolutions. One, from the AUEW, directly rejected United Kingdom membership and committed the Party to withdrawal. The other, from the Boilermakers was a composite resolution supported by Douglas Jay, Chairman of the Labour Committee for Safeguards on the Common Market, a body which reflected the opinions of such anti-Marketeers as Mikardo, Foot, Jay, Shore and Peart. Before the Conference it was reported that Harold Wilson would be well satisfied with any Conference decision, or series of decisions, however conflicting, so long as the National Executive statement was carried. In other words he wanted the Party to unite behind the strategy of renegotiation followed by a General Election or a referendum.

On 4 October at the Conference the NEC statement was carried by a majority of 1,605,000. The engineering motion was defeated by a majority of 180,000. The composite motion was passed but only by a majority of 468,000 votes. (Jack Jones and the TGWU abstained after talks with Wilson). Thus the NEC statement was the most widely accepted policy and Wilson had retained his manouvreability. He said in his speech to the Conference that no other resolution adequately provides that the 'British people have the last word, the right of self-determination which Norway, Denmark and Ireland have had, and which we have said the British people must have.'

The policy of the 1973 Party Conference, on which all the Party united, and of the February and October 1974 Election manifestos, had, then, been established in its essentials in 1972—a commitment to renegotiate and put the terms to the British people. In 1973 Wilson again fended off any move to commit the Party to outright rejection of the EEC. A hard line motion of opposition in principle to the Market was narrowly defeated.

In November 1973 Roy Jenkins rejoined the Shadow Cabinet. The Common Market, though raised strongly by Enoch Powell, was clearly not *the* major issue at the 1974 February Election which, it is interesting to note, the Government chose almost to make a referendum on its policy towards the miners' pay claim. Labour was returned as a minority government and, after the ensuing election in October which gave Labour a minute overall majority, renegotiations on Britain's membership began. The Labour Manifesto of October 1974 had pledged a Labour Government to 'give the British people the final say, which will be binding on the Government—through the ballot box—on whether we accept the terms and stay in or reject the terms and come out.' Clearly a third General Election was not likely, and in addition this would not resolve the continuing division within the Party on the issue. Thus on 23 February 1975 Harold Wilson confirmed that a referendum would be held, probably in June.

We have come to the referendum by way of internal difficulties in the Labour Party. The failure however to present entry into the EEC as a clear issue between the major parties at elections has illustrated once again the deficiencies of the party system. Since at least the days of Joseph Chamberlain the party system has been under criticism and efforts to supplement it have been continuous. The EEC debate illustrates a common failing. The division of opinion is not between the parties but within them. This is also apparent on other issues. We shall return to this subject later.

2 Direct Democracy and the British Tradition

The Party and Parliamentary system as it exists today developed in the 19th century. It has never been a two-party system but until recently it has usually been a two-bloc system. In the days when the Liberal Party was one of the two main parties in the country the Irish, and later the small Labour Party, usually co-operated with it. It should also be said that the Liberal Party went out of its way to make this co-operation possible. The refusal of the present two largest parties to so-operate with smaller parties is one of the difficulties in the present situation.

The system worked satisfactorily so long as the two blocs had on the whole different views upon the main issues of politics. This was the case so long as the issues were such as home rule for Ireland, the role of the State and protection versus free trade. But even before the end of the last century Joseph Chamberlain had made an effort to cut across the division of the parties. Since at least 1910 there has been a continuous effort to break down the traditional party divisions and form a third party.

Now on several of the most important issues before the country, such as defence, nationalization and home rule for Scotland and Wales, the Parties are divided internally. The division on the Common Market, therefore, is only one major example of a growing tendency. Now that the parties themselves are divided on so many issues, the full debate of these issues is obscured and the public have little opportunity for expressing their views.

In any event, under the traditional English system the role of Parliament has lain in questioning, criticizing and checking an executive. The British, following the English system, have never elected an executive directly. Indeed, part of every executive (Cabinet) is still appointed from a non-elected Assembly (the House of Lords). The House of Commons is not in a true sense a legislature. It initiates little legislation itself. This system of somewhat negative democracy worked well so long as the role of government was narrow. Now, however, that government is engaged in ever-widening managerial undertakings the system is in urgent need of reform.

At the same time too the commitments of the electors to political ideology has been weakened. The two-bloc system depended to some extent upon a majority of the electors feeling that they could entrust their representation to the Liberal or Conservative Parties right across the spectrum of politics. Now, very few of the voters feels wholly committed to one party on all its policies. The present situation in the House of Commons is that there are now six parties, all operating separately. The party in Government commanded only 38% of the votes at the Election. The Liberal Party obtained over 5 million votes and only got 13 seats.

Against this background it can be seen that it is not only because of the controversy over remaining in the EEC that the British should be examining their political system.

It is noteworthy that of all the major areas of our national life the political system has been the most resistant to change. It is true that, in comparison with the past, the last decade or so saw many attempts at reform, but it is already clear that such developments as did take place were both too little and too late. The creation of specialized committees has not managed to re-vitalize Parliament as their advocates had hoped. The outlook and practices of the Civil Service and the advice which it tenders to ministers have not noticeably improved despite the recommendations of the Fulton Report. The amalgamation of government functions into vast 'federal' ministries with their teams of ministers and extra permanent secretaries cannot be said to have improved the performance of the executive branch of government in any visible way. The appointment of an Ombudsman, while welcome in principle, has made only a very limited impact on the conduct of Whitehall because his powers have been very circumscribed. The one full-blooded reform—that of local government—creating elephantine, remote and costly authorities has already proved to be inefficient and unpopular.

Equally there has been a reluctance on the part of both Labour and Conservative governments to face up boldly to the issue of home rule for Scotland and Wales and to the pressing need to bring about a drastic devolution of central government powers. Mainstream politics and the central institutions of government remain much as they have always been. The old shiboleths, such as the principle of ministerial responsibility and the doctrine of collective Cabinet responsibility, are still bandied about though in practice they are adhered to less and less. This state of affairs is inevitable until a thorough going examination of our constitutional requirements is made in the light of contemporary conditions which will propose new ideas and principles for the conduct of government, which will surely include schemes for greater public participation in decision making.

The Absence of a Tradition of Direct Democracy in Britain

Why is it that in comparison with most other western nations, and others elsewhere in the world, that Britain has generally avoided recourse to forms of direct democracy?

Much of the reason is rooted in the fact that Britain is unique in having a long tradition of strong, highly centralized government. In some countries provision for direct democracy resulted from an early tradition of localities deciding their own affairs through town or canton meetings. Since the Wars of the Roses, at any rate, this has not been the experience of Britain.

Only in England has the parliamentary assembly had a continuous history from the middle ages to the present time. The crucial problems involved in the development of most states, such as the creation of a central government, the definition of the political community, and the relationship of Church and State were resolved separately and in piecemeal fashion in England: at no time did they cause a breakdown in the acceptance or legitimacy of the government. Indeed one of the present authors recalls that on a visit to this country some fifteen years ago General de Gaulle stated his opinion that the most remarkable feature of British government was its legitimacy.

Thus settlements of what have been called the 'great crises of cultural development' were arrived at in Britain prior to the industrial and political upheavals which began in the late eighteenth century. Furthermore, the slow transition between feudal and bourgeois orders, with the consequent widening of the ruling classes to include new interests, was achieved peacefully and gradually in Britain. The emerging commercial interests were assimilated into the existing scheme of political representation. They did not, as elsewhere, have to challenge fundamentally the old order by claiming to speak for 'the people'. In France, on the other hand, the new interests, faced with an intransigent regime, justified their overthrowing it by reference to a belief in the 'general will' of the people and a commitment to direct democracy. Because of Britain's gradual political

29

development, and the concomitant sustaining of the legitimacy of both the government and the system of representation on which it was based, a plebiscitary tradition never became established.

In some countries which utilize forms of direct democracy, these often exist alongside a representative system. This is frequently the case where there is a written constitution which provides for the use of referenda as a special device to be used for amending the constitution. In such cases a distinction is usually made between the constitutional and the ordinary law of the land, whereby the former is subject to a special legislative procedure. The constitution—the legal framework of rules by which the political system operates—is thus 'entrenched': special processes are necessary to change it, and these often include a direct appeal to the people to either accept or reject proposed amendments. Many of Britain's former colonies adopted constitutions embodying such conditions, especially where they were considered necessary to protect the interests of ethnic, religious or tribal minorities in the newly independent states.

We will examine the use of referenda for this purpose in detail in the next chapter. The point to be made here, however, is that Britain has no written constitution and no distinction between ordinary and constitutional law; in the making of all law Parliament (or technically the Queen-in-Parliament) is legally sovereign. This absence of a written constitution reflects the long history of centralized government in England and Britain.

Centralized 'representative' government not only maintained sufficient consent to ward off challenges to its legitimacy, but also it was sufficiently efficient and open to make it difficult to challenge on the grounds of corruption. The direct democracy movement in the American States at the turn of the century reflected the strong feeling against the corruption of state government at that time. State legislatures dominated by special interests were unfavourably contrasted to the direct and incorruptable voice of the people.

In this context it is interesting to note that the English parish is an ancient exception to the centralizing tendencies of our system of government, and one which provides for a measure of direct democracy. The parish as a unit with administrative functions, in addition to its ecclesiastical role, can be traced back to medieval times. In the reign of Elizabeth I it was given the task of dealing with vagrancy and poverty relief. The Local Government Act, 1894 made statutory provision in England and Wales for the holding of parish meetings in all rural districts and for the creation of parish councils in the more populous areas. Over 7000 parishes were designated. The parish meeting has to be called at least once a year and, like the Anglo-Saxon tun moot, consists of all the electors of the parish. The recent reform of local government, creating very large local authorities, has provoked a suggestion that the parish system should be extended to urban areas in the form of local neighbourhood councils to offset the remoteness of the larger authorities. This is but one of many examples of the new wave of participatory thinking which has emerged in recent years and which, if it gathers enough popular momentum, may well lead to a substantial modification or even radical reform of the highly centralized system of government.

The Tradition of Political Representation in Britain
Representatives rule in Britain. They rule in the knowledge that, though given authority to act in what they see as the best interests of the nation, they must sooner or later face the country at a General Election. They rule not in the sense that the House of Commons itself makes laws, or could do so—but in the sense that it supports, and will generally go on supporting, a Government. In modern

times the convention has been that the Party which gains, at an election, a majority of seats in the Commons forms a Government: the Government can thus count (in normal circumstances) on approval for its acts by the Commons.

The Government actually makes law, but the system can still be described as representative in several senses:

i   Firstly, it is composed of Members of Parliament. Bagehot talked in this sense of the fusion between the Cabinet, (the executive), and Parliament, (the legislature).

II Secondly, it is in some ways responsible to Parliament between elections.

iii Thirdly, in the way we described above, it derives its power through Parliament, by virtue of its control over a majority of the MPs.

This system of political representation has been based on a number of established principles.

First, as mentioned earlier, no distinction has been made in Britain between constitutional and ordinary law. Parliament is legally sovereign in its ability to make and alter law, and the preservation of this right has been one of the main planks in the arguements of such anti-marketeers as Michael Foot and Enoch Powell. Thus Parliament, with a normal majority vote, can extend the duration of itself as it did during the Second World War, or suspend normal civil liberties by introducing internment, as it has done in wartime and most recently in Ulster. The checks which exist to prevent abuse in such cases are essentially informal ones.

Secondly, laws are in no circumstances submitted to the people for their endorsement through referenda or similar devices. Instead the government is generally left free to govern, subject to the scrutiny of Parliament, according to what it feels to be are the best interests of the country, subject to the knowledge that it must face the electorate at periodic elections. It is in this sense that British government is described as being 'responsible' government: its virtually sole responsibility being in no way qualified by arrangements which require its proposals to have prior popular approval or subsequent ratification.

A third, and much discussed, principle is that of the role of the MP. The orthodox view was enunciated long before the arrival of mass democracy and never more clearly than by Edmund Burke in his letter to the voters of Bristol in 1774:

> 'You choose a member, indeed; but when you have chosen him, he is not member of Bristol, but he is a member of *Parliament*. If the local constituent should have an interest or should form an hasty opinion evidently opposite to the real good of the rest of the community, the member for that place ought to be as far as any other from any endeavour to give it effect.'

According to Burke, then, the MP is the representative rather than the delegate of his constituency. Though it is sometimes challenged, this view has predominated against all others. Indeed, it is used by those pro-marketeer MPs who are strongly opposed to the EEC Referendum; of course they accept that the MP must take popular opinion into account in making up his own mind on a particular issue, but in the end it is his responsibility to cast his vote in Parliament as he thinks fit. Public opinion, the advocates of the MP as representative principle argue, can be very fickle and reactionary: the task of the MP is to lead rather than to follow the electorate. If an MP diverges too much from the views of his constituents then they are at liberty to unseat him at the next election.

What links these two levels, and complicates this picture of the independent, free thinking representative, is the party system. The tradition remains that MPs should not merely follow their constituents wishes—assuming they spoke with one voice. But instead of exercising free choice, the modern MP follows—in normal circumstances—the line of his party. In the major parties the MP is elected not because of his individual attitudes but because he has been nominated as the official candidate of one or other of the parties. People vote for the party not the man. Thus the MP, ,once elected, will generally support either the Government in office—if his party is in office—or the Opposition.

It is because MPs generally vote with their parties that responsible government has been possible. The Government can act independently, supported by its party majority in the Commons, and subject only to the electorate's subsequent verdict. The Government can be held fully accountable *because* it can count on a majority in Parliament. It is interesting in this context to note the contrast between the British Parliament and the American Congress. The American Congressman is much more of a delegate, and the party system is that much weaker. It is the President in the American system who represents the general interest: he is elected separately and directly by all the people. In the American system responsibility is sometimes hard to allocate because of the shared nature of powers between the Presidency and Congress. Each branch can and does deny final responsibility on the grounds that its actions were impeded by the activities of the other branch. No such excuses exist for a British government in the normal course of events.

Thus the Burkean dictum remains the guiding principle, although the idea of the modern party was then unknown. The issue still arises when MPs take a stand in Parliament which conflicts with the views of their party colleagues in the House or with their constituency parties. On the Suez invasion several Conservative MPs came under attack from their constituency parties for voting against their government in the Commons. The most celebrated rebel, as it turned out, was Nigel Nicolson. His local party voted not to re-adopt him to fight the next election, but after a good deal of negotiation Conservative Central Office persuaded the local party to hold a poll of all its members to decide the question of Nicolson's re-adoption. The result of this mini-referendum was a narrow victory in favour of the MP, who nevertheless decided not to stand.

More recently, because of his stand on the EEC, the Lincoln Labour party decided to drop the sitting MP, Dick Taverne, as their candidate. He held the seat fighting as an independent Social Democrat at the election of February 1974 but lost it at the election held the following October.

Adverse constituency opinion is an important factor in re-inforcing adherence to strict party voting by MPs in the two largest parties. An additional factor pulling in the same direction is that junior ministerial office is usually given to those who loyally toe the official line, although as the careers of Churchill, Eden and Wilson illustrate rebellion does not preclude a politician from ascending to the top of the 'greasy pole' as the ministerial hierarchy has been aptly called.

Generally, however, most members are happy to support the party line. Politics has traditionally been conducted in this fashion, particularly in the post-war period: issues have either fallen into, or else have been pushed into, the conventional categories of Left or Right. The system, in the past at any rate, gained Britain a reputation for strong government.

These, then, were the 'rules of the political game' as they have been played out for most of the last hundred years, excluding National Governments, occasional and short lived minority governments and periods when one party is replacing another—as the Liberal Party was 'replaced' by the Labour Party in the 1920s. Some of these rules are already in decline; others have been challenged. We are not arguing that this is the best system, only that these have been the general principles on which modern representative and responsible government in this country has been based. It is, of course, a tradition which is antagonistic towards any form of direct democracy.

One principle, however, we have not mentioned, is that of the 'mandate'. It can be said for both parties that in voting for a Labour or Conservative candidate at an election the voter is giving the successful candidate a mandate to support his party in Parliament either to keep the Government in office, or to support the Opposition. After all, people vote for the party, not the man. Similarly a new Government may claim a mandate to govern. But here the traditions in the two main parties differ, or seem to differ considerably. In a system which stresses responsible government with a retrospective consent by the electorate, there is an internal contradiction. This contradiction is provided by the doctrine of the mandate as it has developed in the Labour Party.

The Labour Party and the Doctrine of the Mandate
As we said earlier, political parties on gaining a majority of seats in the House of Commons, following a general election, can and do claim a 'mandate to govern'. The meaning of this term, however, differs in the Conservative and Labour parties. If the Burkean theory is applied to government and not to MPs, the theory is consistent with the internal rules, constitution and traditional conduct of the Conservative party. It is a hierarchical party, born in Parliament, which created a mass organization outside Parliament in the 1860s to organize the newly enfranchised voters.

The mass organization of the Tories originated simply to support the Conservatives in Parliament and, in the

36

main, it has continued to play this secondary role. The Conservative Leader is granted considerable authority in the party and is not obliged—under the party's constitution—to do more than take note of the views of the party in the country, the National Union, or the Parliamentary party; though he would be well advised to pay due heed to them as Edward Heath learnt to his cost. Furthermore, the Leader appoints the head of the party organization, the Central Office. Not only is the Leader dominant in day to day affairs, but he also controls the drawing up of the party's election manifesto. He can pledge the party to as much or as little as he thinks fit. Traditionally, this has not been much. Conservatives have generally avoided detailed policy or programme commitments and have interpreted a mandate as giving the government a general grant of authority to act day to day in the best interests of the nation. The government is later held to account for how it has exercised this authority at a subsequent election. But the bestowal or the withholding of approval by the electorate, it is important to stress, is retrospective.

There is nothing, then, in the formal way in which the Conservatives conduct themselves which conflicts with the tenets of the British constitution as it has developed in modern times. And much the same could be said of the Liberal Party's arrangements whether it has been in or out of office.

How far the Labour Party fits into this scheme of things has always been a matter of contention. The notion of the mandate, which is very important in the formal system of the party and in much of the rhetoric of its leading members, is usually taken to refer to the practice of delegation which is part and parcel of Labour's system of internal party democracy. As such this notion of the mandate constitutes a rather different, and later, theory of representation than that subscribed to by Liberals and

Conservatives which theoretically is at variance with the strictest interpretation of British constitutional practice. The reason why the Labour Party diverges from the other two older parties is rooted in its history for, unlike them, it developed first as an extra-parliamentary movement which only subsequently gained seats in Parliament. Thus, under the Party Constitution Labour's annual conference is charged with deciding the policy of the Party, and between conferences policy is determined and interpreted by the National Executive Committee, (NEC) whose members are elected by the conference.

The Party's election manifesto is jointly written by the Parliamentary leadership (the Cabinet or Shadow Cabinet as the case may be) and the NEC. A Labour Leader, therefore, is continually faced with the problem of dealing with a separate and co-equal (and officially superior) source of power in the Party in the form of the conference and the NEC which it spawns, but he does not have a free hand in deciding the electoral programme of the Party. A strong, if not universally held, feeling in the Labour Party is that the manifesto, worked out by the parliamentary leadership in conjunction with the NEC representing the party at large is binding on a Labour government when elected. Rather than giving a Labour government and its Leader a general mandate of authority to govern, election victory is seen as commiting and mandating the new government to the programme spelt out in the manifesto. Furthermore, since no programme can predict future eventualities, both the annual conference and the NEC will continually seek to assert their authroity on the Cabinet throughout the life of the government.

However broadly the two British traditions (Conservative/Liberal and Labour) are drawn, the distinct difference in philosophy and organization is clear. Within the British system of representation, which was basically 'a descending theory of representation' with

38

power flowing downwards from the top, there exists a party with a rather different theory. This is less antagonistic towards the principles of direct democracy: that is to say that the Labour Party is organized on 'an ascending theory of representation', whereby power and authority flows from the bottom up both in the sense of the constitutional distribution of power within the Party and in the sense of the electorate's 'mandating' act of voting Labour into office.

The orthodox view amongst experts is that the formal constitutional and theoretical differences between the political parties matters little in practice. They argue that, for the most part, the Labour Party draws back from implementing the full letter of its constitution particularly when it is in office, so that in the event a Labour government adheres to the principles of the British constitution as faithfully as a Conservative one. Moreover, they argue that this validates their view that the actual distribution of power in the two main parties, despite the formal rubric to the contrary, is much more similar than different. The evidence which is usually used to validate this view is the ease with which Clement Attlee dismissed the demand of Harold Laski —the chairman of the NEC in 1945—for the NEC to be closely consulted by the prime minister in the formulation of Cabinet policy. This interpretation may have been true in the past but it may not square so easily with reality in the future.

The rather dismal record of the 1964-70 Labour Government, culminating in its surprise defeat by the Conservatives, seems to have engendered a generally felt greater determination to implement party policy more faithfully than previously and to develop closer collaboration between the parliamentary leadership, the NEC and its industrial wing and original progenitor the TUC. Greater emphasis has been placed on the content of the manifesto of the party. Indeed, in the election of

October 1974 Harold Wilson stressed in his campaigning how much of the manifesto, on which the Party had fought the election held the previous February, had already been fulfilled by the Labour government. The manifesto and the mandate are having a greater impact on the conduct of Labour in office—at least so far.

An even more interesting development is the way in which the Conservative party has been changing over the past decade or so. First, after the furore over the emergence of Lord Home as Leader in 1963 it decided to emulate the practice of Labour (and the Liberals for that matter) and to elect its Leader in future. In 1974 it went even further and adopted the principle of annual elections for the leadership based on a system resembling a variant of proportional representation. Power still resides firmly within the parliamentary party but the Leader is now regarded as being less than omnipotent.

Secondly, the Conservatives seem, albeit rather haltingly, to be moving closer to the Labour practice of drawing up detailed and specific policy programmes for submission to the electorate. This happened first in the run up to the 1970 election when the party presented itself, in what was dubbed its 'Selsdon Man' guise, as being committed to implementing a more full-blooded capitalistic programme than had been the case for many a year. The old economic consensus of 'Butskellism' was to be abandoned. As it turned out the Heath government lost its nerve after about a year and reverted to a more middle-of-the-road approach. Enoch Powell refused to fight the following election on the specific grounds that he could not stand for a party and a Leader who had so flagrantly renaged on the previous manifesto. Again under Mrs Thatcher the Conservatives are preparing to produce distinctively Conservative plans for a 'social market' (i.e. more capitalistic) economy which will constitute the main plank of her election platform next time.

The greater emphasis which is being placed on manifestos by both parties is being made in response to the growing lack of credibility in parties and politicians on the part of the general public. It is an attempt to *increase rapport* between the party and the electorate and to improve the morale of the rank-and-file members of the party. This increased stress on the manifesto, coupled with a greater determination to implement its contents, is indicative of the way in which British politics is moving away from the accepted notions of representative democracy towards a more participatory style. The holding of a referendum on Britain's EEC membership is a further step in this direction.

The orthodox view of the operations of a modern and mature democracy is that the affairs of state are altogether too complex to be comprehended by ordinary people. Thus it follows, so it is argued, that the citizen's role must be confined to choosing between the competing parties at periodic elections. This view has been proved wrong in at least two major respects. First, the problems of modern government have patently proved to be beyond the understanding of politicians and bureaucratic experts alike, so that they do not have a monopoly of wisdom. Secondly, as this fact becomes apparent, ordinary people so-called are increasingly refusing to accept the limited role of periodic elector. Hence the growing recourse to forms of direct action such as the 'work ins' at Upper Clyde Shipbuilders, Meriden, and the Imperial Typewriter factories, and the blockade of ports and harbours by fishermen.

There is a third objection to the orthodox view. What happens if, after the electors have dutifully cast their votes, the final result is either indecisive or returns governments with very narrow majorities in Parliament based on a minority vote in the country at large? Three out of the last five elections held in Britain, those of 1964

41

and the two held ten years later, have hardly been conclusive. When this happens the legitimacy of the government is impaired and its 'right' to govern severely qualified. This situation makes strong government difficult to achieve. The old, so-called 'two party system' is being visibly erroded. Parties are unable to mobilize anything approaching majority support: the Labour party's share of the poll in 1964 was 44.1%, by February 1974 it had fallen to 37.1%. When this situation arises in other countries, as is frequently the case, there is a greater tendency towards the formation of coalition governments together with some tendency towards forms of greater popular participation including the use of referenda. In otherwords government has to take steps to be more responsive. Given developments that are already in train it may well be that the British system will become more 'responsive' and less 'responsible' in the sense in which it has been used.

Recent Developments Towards Greater Public Participation and Direct Democracy in Britain

It is quite clear that the pattern of British politics has been undergoing significant changes over the past twenty years, and that, both as a cause and as a consequence of these changes, the system of government is being subjected to increasing strains.

The turnout at general elections has been declining gradually, as have the individual memberships of the two largest parties. Political activists, particularly the younger ones, are beginning to turn away from the parties and from parliamentary politics and are concentrating their energies instead into other political channels. The rapid growth in recent years of such pressure groups as Shelter, the Child Poverty Action Group, Friends of the Earth and similar organizations is one very obvious sign of the times. Allied this has been the upsurge in community action.

This has included tenants' campaigns against private and public landlords alike, protests against the siting of the proposed third London airport, demonstrations against motorway developments, squatting in empty accommodation and many other issues which have incenced various groups of citizens. Consumers associations have sprung up both locally and at national level to press their demands for a better deal for the consumer.

These manifestations of direct democracy have met with a good deal of success. Those living near London's Westway have been re-housed, and many local authorities have entered into agreements with local squatters' groups to allow them to use empty premises. The third London airport has been abandoned. The Government has set up an Office of Fair Trading and a National Consumers' Council. Parent-governors are beginning to be appointed to the management boards of schools. The Stop-the-Seventy-Tour contributed to preventing the South African cricketers from touring the country. Firms and local authorities have now to be more aware of ecological and environmental considerations as a result of the activities of conservationist groups.

Parallel to the above developments changes have been taking place in the industrial field. The trade union movement, for much of its history, has incorporated forms of participation for its rank and file members in the constitutions of many of its individual unions. In unions such as the Mineworkers for example, ballots (referenda) of the entire membership have to be held to sanction official strike action and to call it off. Many unions ballot their members to approve or reject pay deals negotiated with employers. Again, most unions base their system of internal representation on the principle of local branches sending mandated delegates to the national conferences. The low level of rank and file participation in union affairs, pay and strike ballots excepted, has led on occasions to the system being abused as in the case of the Electrical Trades Union some years ago. It is perhaps not surprising, therefore, that the national leaderships of the unions are finding it difficult always to retain the loyalty of their members. In recent years there has been a noticeable shift of power away from the national leaders to the local shop stewards as evidenced by the very high number of unofficial strikes and stoppages. Growing shopfloor militancy has lately given rise to the new phenomenon of 'work ins', whereby workers have taken over the factories whenever their livelihood has been threatened. As a result of these tactics the present government has agreed to finance workers' co-operatives to run factories which otherwise would have closed at Kirkby and Meriden. Support for a similar scheme has been promised to help launch the *Scottish Daily News,* which is to be run by the former employees of the now defunct *Scottish Daily Express.*

Important clauses in Tony Benn's Industry Bill and Michael Foot's Employment Protection Bill, both of which should reach the statute book in 1975, extend the rights of trade unions to have company information made available to them as of right. These provisions will undoubtedly increase the opportunities for trade unions to participate in the decisions taken by companies. An even further step towards participation is foreshadowed in the Ryder Report on British Leyland which recommends that employee representatives should have a voice in the running of the company.

Not all the recent examples of popular discontent are to be welcomed. Nevertheless, some exceptions apart, there is no doubt that there is a groundswell of popular feeling in favour of greater participation and for a larger measure of direct democracy to complement the traditional system of parliamentary representation. In the light of this the decision to hold a referendum on whether Britain should remain in the Common Market is wholly in tune with the new participatory mood. It would be a mistake in our view to regard the Referendum as being solely the result of the divisions over the EEC within the Labour Party important as these are. Certainly these divisions have played a large part in deciding to hold a referendum, but the decision should also be seen in the context of the changes which have been taking place in the political and industrial life of the country. Though the success of these developments should not be exaggerated. So far they have been largely peripheral. On the whole the bureaucratic attitude is still advancing at the expense of the democratic.

The Referendum in British Political History

Despite what is said about Britain's continuous history of strong and stable government, major political crises have occurred from time to time. In the light of these it is surprising that the EEC issue is the first time that a national referendum has been actually used for resolving a crisis and it is worthwhile to take a closer look at the reasons for this; as we shall see referenda have been seriously considered in the past.

Referenda have not been resorted to in Britain before because crises have usually been solved by general elections. Such crisis elections have generally produced a large majority for one party, and thus a government with an electors' mandate to take the necessary steps to resolve the problem.

Two elections which failed to produce clear majorities, however, were those of 1910. The first, held on the issue of the 'people versus the peers' was intended to resolve the problem of the obstruction by the House of Lords of the reforms—notably the 'people's Budget' of 1909—of the new Liberal Government. In fact the Conservatives gained seats, and in the period of deadlock which resulted the idea of a referendum was first mooted. A. J. Balfour, the

Conservative leader, proposed that any important Bill passed by the Commons but defeated in the Lords should be submitted to a referendum. He added that he would accept a referendum on tariff reform, an issue on which the party was divided.

The Liberals, however, held a second general election in November 1910 which produced virtually no change. They then introduced a Parliament Bill to greatly reduce the power of the House of Lords. Some Conservatives (using an argument similar to that used by Conservatives in Denmark in 1953) argued that if this check and 'opportunity for second thoughts' was to be lost, it should be replaced by one of equal value, namely the referendum. However, with the final passage of the Parliament Act in 1911 the crisis subsided and the referendum issue died.

The idea of the referendum again became part of Conservative policy over the issue of food tariffs in 1930. A strong element of the party, led by Lord Beaverbrook, were campaigning—using the deceptive slogan of Empire Free Trade—for the adoption of a policy supporting tariffs. In March 1930, under pressure from Beaverbrook, Baldwin decided to support the idea of a referendum on the issue. Before holding such a referendum a Conservative Government would first call an Empire Conference, so that the economic advantages of the tariffs could be demonstrated; (there are shades here of the Labour Party's renegotiations followed by a referendum pledge in 1972). The argument was also used that food tariffs would be a constitutional change, and so justify a unique procedure.

Beaverbrook began to feel that the leadership of the Party was using the referendum device in order to avoid the issue of food taxes, rather than to promote it. At an Imperial Conference in 1930 the Canadian Prime Minister proposed an increase in duties and this led to a falling off of interest in the issue and the abandonment of the referendum idea.

A final instance of a referendum being proposed by a Conservative Party leader came in May 1945, in a letter written by Prime Minister Winston Churchill to C. R. Attlee. Churchill suggested that a referendum might be held in order to legitimize a continuation of the war-time coalition until the defeat of Japan. In reply Attlee summarily rejected the idea and wrote that referenda were 'alien to our traditions'.

These three instances were clearly exceptional. A referendum was considered in 1910 because of the electoral and constitutional deadlock of that time, while in 1930 Baldwin briefly adopted the idea to conciliate pressure in his party and to move some way towards support for food tariffs. This second instance seems to have most relevance for the 1970's situation.

Post-war elections have until recently generally produced governments with clear majorities, while the parties have resolved differences internally without recourse to referenda. Elections have been held with the clear intention of testing opinion on one issue, but a general election in practice inevitably reflects a number of different factors. The House of Lords issue was dominant in the February 1910 election, while in 1923 Baldwin adopted the policy of protection and decided to hold an election on the issue, an election which was disastrous for the Tories. Finally, in February 1974, sixteen months before he need have gone to the country, Edward Heath held a general election at which his immediate and major argument was his request for support for his policy of resistance to the miners' pay claim.

The earlier instances do show that in exceptional circumstances referenda have been suggested and seriously considered in modern British politics.

The one occasion when a large-scale referendum has

been used in Britain, or a part of it at least—except, that is, for the popular ballots held in Wales to determine local licensing hours for public houses on the Sabbath—was in 1973 when a plebiscite was held in Ulster to decide whether the province should remain an integral part of the United Kingdom or be re-united with the Irish Republic. This, or course, was not a national referendum as is the EEC one, nor, more importantly, did it resolve the crisis in Northern Ireland.

The Case For and Against the British Referendum on the EEC

Chapter I outlined the historical background which led to the decision to hold a referendum to determine whether or not Britain should remain in the EEC. In this chapter, we have analysed why it is that Britain has previously avoided the use of referenda and why, for the most part, it has managed to rely on a system of representative democracy and has largely eschewed schemes based on the principles of direct democracy. We have suggested that the traditional pattern of politics may now be in the process of changing and, furthermore, that this is likely to involve some significant changes in the methods of government. The decision to hold a referendum is itself a reflection of the new developments that are taking place.

In the next chapter we shall look in some detail at the ways in which other countries use referenda, but first it is necessary to examine the arguments which are currently being deployed about the wisdom or otherwise of holding a referendum in Britain on the issue of the EEC. As we shall see, it is not always easy to disentangle the threads of the different arguments.

In the first place, much of the controversy is internal to the Labour party. Although there are significant exceptions, it is nevertheless broadly true that the referendum issue has split the party along left-right lines.

48

Thus the anti-marketeers, of which the Tribune Group has emerged as the main force, tend to be on the left wing of the party, while the pro-marketeers come in the main from Labour's right wing and centre. To further complicate matters the anti-marketeers generally support the idea of using the referendum while the pro-marketeers are opposed to it. Although Harold Wilson ultimately accepted the use of the referendum as the solution least likely to perpetuate the rift in the party over the EEC, the task of re-uniting the party after the outcome is known will not be an easy one, particularly as the issue has polarized along left-right lines. Disagreements between the two wings of the party as to the best means for dealing with the country's economic problems, which have widened since Denis Healey's April budget, will add further to the dissentions in the party.

If the Referendum results in a popular majority against Britain remaining in the EEC, a leading Labour pro-marketeer, Shirley Williams—the Secretary of State for Prices and Consumer Protection—is on record that she will retire from public life. Following a negative vote it is difficult to see how the main Labour pro-marketeer, Roy Jenkins—the Home Secretary—could remain in the Cabinet, while the position of James Callaghan as Foreign Secretary (and the person primarily responsible for re-negotiating Britain's terms of membership of the EEC) would be almost untenable.

If the Referendum produces a majority in favour of staying in the EEC, it will be a severe defeat for the left wing of the party, but conceivably it will be less damaging to Labour unity in the long run. A major reason for suggesting this is that the main anti-market protagonists, and in particular Tony Benn, have publicly undertaken to abide by the public's decision. In these circumstances they will have to lick their wounds and concentrate on other issues to press their cause.

Whatever the decision after 5 June, if the Labour party is faced with a long, drawn out crisis of unity, the implications of it will be felt well beyond the confines of the party. Should such a situation materialize, it will be tempting for those who disagreed with the use of the referendum to claim that history has proved them right. Such a conclusion would be too facile, for no one can say what the consequences would have been for Labour had another course been chosen in an attempt to resolve the question of the EEC.

The main objection to a referenda is that they are foreign to the precepts of the parliamentary system of government. Those who argue this way fear that it will undermine, perhaps irrevocably, the sovereignty of Parliament and that the very legitimacy of the system will be called into question. It is further argued that once the precedent has been established it will be difficult to resist demands for referenda on other subjects. This point was made by Roy Jenkins in his letter of resignation as Deputy Leader of the Labour party in April 1972, following the shadow cabinet's decision to support the call for a referendum. To those who argued that it would be a once-and-for-all event, he countered that once 'the principle of the Referendum has been introduced into British politics it will not rest with any one party to put a convenient limit on its use'. Opponents of a referenda also claim that the regular mobilization of public opinion by such means may well result in more reactionary legislation on certain issues than would be the case if they were left simply to the deliberations of Parliament: minorities will be exposed to the tyranny of the brute majority.

Allied to this last point is the argument, heard less now perhaps than in the past, that a referendum takes no account of the quality or intensity of feeling on an issue. A head count may disguise a mildly committed majority and an impassioned minority. In short, those who dislike referenda prefer representative to direct democracy. They believe that MPs are a better medium for reconciling differences and gauging the intensity of popular feelings.

The advocates of the Referendum mainly base their case on the fact that membership of the EEC so threatens our national independence and the sovereignty of parliament that so profound a constitutional change must be referred to the people. Thus we have the rather bewildering situation, generally speaking, that the pro-marketeers are in favour of a modification of parliamentary sovereignty by transferring some powers to the EEC, but will countenance no breach of the self-same sovereignty in the form of a referendum. Contrariwise, the anti-marketeers will fight to the last to protect parliamentary sovereignty against encroachment from the EEC, but will happily dispense with it in favour of a referendum.

How then do we assess the arguments that the use of the referendum is likely to undermine representative government, with harmful consequences? Much depends on whether the Common Market issue is accepted as a 'special case'. Certainly the division in the Labour Party on this issue, highlighting as it does the separate power centres within the Party, especially in opposition, was and is of very high intensity. As of April 1975 the Parliamentary Party is almost exactly split between pro and anti-marketeers. No issue since the 1930s has so divided a major Party.

So far only Tony Benn has ever suggested the possibility of using referenda more widely. The one issue on which it seems some demand for a referenda can be expected is that of Welsh and Scottish home rule or independence. If British electors have been given the right to adjudicate on closer association with the nations of the EEC can the Scots or the Welsh be denied the same right to decide whether or not to remain within the United Kingdom? Here, of course, the precedent is not so much the EEC

51

Referendum but the plebiscite held in Northern Ireland.

What effect the EEC referendum will have in the eyes of the public on the legitimacy of subsequent parliamentary legislation it is difficult to say (though legitimacy has not always been accorded in large enough measure to permit the enforcement of laws in the past, as illustrated by the old betting laws and more recently by the Conservative's Industrial Relations Act). So long as the system of government is responsive and effective there is unlikely to be any widespread rejection of laws passed by Parliament as some fear.

A rash of referenda is equally unlikely. In normal circumstances governments will not have an interest in 'Passing the buck'. A greater use of referenda is likely to depend on the extent to which new issues arise which result in unbridgeable divisions within the political parties. A government's electoral considerations are a strong counter incentive against the development of such divisions. If such issues emerge, however, cutting across party lines to a degree that 'passing the buck' to the people is the only way out for a government, then this will show that the parties themselves are becoming inadequate vehicles to deal with modern problems. That is to say, if referenda are used more widely in the future in Britain, with the consequent reduction in the responsibility and accountability of MPs and governments alike, this will be a reflection of profound political changes of which the EEC issue is but one manifestation.

3   Foreign Experience of the Referendum

1   Introduction

What is a referendum? Generally we see it as the act, practice or principle of submitting the direct decision of a question at issue to the whole body of voters. A referendum can thus clearly be distinguished from an election, at which the voters choose between individuals or parties. But just as in a true election it is generally accepted that the voters should be given a real alternative, so a proper referendum should offer a real alternative to the voters. In most referenda voters are asked to decide YES or NO on the question at issue, but some have asked the electorate to choose between a number of choices.

To us a pure referendum has two other implications. Firstly, that the question on the ballot paper is the real question which the voters are deciding. Secondly, that the result of the Referendum will either be binding on the Government or will at least be given great weight by the Government in making its own decision.

Before looking at some examples it is worth trying to distinguish a plebiscite from a referendum, although at times the words have been used interchangeably. The dictionary definition of a plebiscite is as follows:

> In modern politics, a direct vote of the whole of the electors of a state to decide a question of public importance; also by extension, a public expression, with or without binding force, of the wishes or opinions of the community.

The extention indicates the broader scope of a plebiscite,

covering general expressions of public opinion not restricted to a 'question at issue'. The dividing line is not clear, but some idea of the difference can be obtained by examining several examples.

On 12 November 1933, for example, German voters were faced with having to answer YES or NO to the following question:

> Do you German man and you German woman approve the policy of your Government, and are you ready to declare it as an expression of your own opinion and of your own will and solemnly adhere to it?

Although no mention was made of it in the question, the vote followed the decision by Hitler in the autumn of 1933 to withdraw German participation in the League of Nations and the Disarmament Conference. Hitler clearly wanted his action to be given legitimacy by a mass vote of the German people. This indeed was the result:

YES	40,588,804
NO	2,100,181
Votes polled	43,439,046
Spoiled	750,001

The YES vote was approximately 95%. The poll was preceded by a violent propaganda campaign by the Nazis. Rather than being a delegation of power to the electorate to decide a clearly defined question, the authorities were using the poll to get a blanket endorsement of their policy and to strengthen the position of the regime both internally and internationally.

Hitler used this device several times. In 1934 he gained retrospective approval for his decision to have all presidential powers transferred to him as President and Fuhrer. Later. the occupation of the Rhineland (in 1936) and the seizure of Austria (in 1938) were put to the people for approval in the same way, and the results used to intimidate other countries from opposing German expansion.

In these instances the poll decides nothing. The poll gives the people the opportunity of expressing their acclaim of the Government and that is its purpose. Hitler's plebiscites were in the tradition of those used by the Napoleons in France in the nineteenth century. In 1802 three and a half million Frenchmen (with only eight thousand opposed) approved the proposal of making Napoleon I consul for life. When Napoleon III executed his coup d'etat in 1851 he ordered a plebiscite to be held on the question of whether the French people approved of his action. 7,439,216 people voted in affirmation, with only 640,737 voting in the negative. Here again the plebiscite was retrospective; no result could alter the fact of Napoleon's rule.

To say that recent French referenda have conformed more to what we have described as the plebiscitary tradition, than to that of the referendum is not to equate de Gaulle's France with Hitler's Germany.* The danger of a plebiscite is that a leader can appeal over the heads of parliament, interests and parties to seek a direct mandate in the popular will. If the leader can also control the media of communication, and can suppress opposition, then the plebiscite becomes a means of one-man dictatorship. The situation in France has been quite different from Germany in the 1930s, there being a strong tradition of liberty and freedom of speech. It should also be pointed out that President de Gaulle resigned in 1969

---

* It should be pointed out that there is also a separate tradition of plebiscites in which genuine decisions have been made. These were the votes of self determination, in which the people of various disputed territories decided to attach themselves to one or another nation. A number of plebiscites were held under the 1918 Peace Treaty, including those in Northern Schleswig, East Prussia, Upper Silesia, and the Saar Valley.

when his proposals to the French voters were rejected by a referendum. He lived by direct democracy—using it to legitimize his authority as President of the Republic—and he also 'died' by it.

We shall discuss the recent French referenda later, but it seems to us that they have more in common with some American presidential elections than with classical Swiss referenda. They have to do not with a decision on one issue, but with the general legitimacy of the regime and with its mandate to govern. Particularly at times of crisis, this legitimacy is crucial. In 1932 in America a new, large majority of American voters gave Franklin D. Roosevelt a mandate to take exceptional steps (thus expanding the generally accepted 'legitimate' role of the government) to cope with a situation of Depression and fifteen million unemployed. An even larger majority confirmed Roosevelt's actions in 1936.

The use of plebiscites in strengthening one-man rule can be illustrated by more recent examples. In 1960, for example, Kwame Nkrumah decided to hold a plebiscite on a new and republican constitution for Ghana, with himself as President. It has been claimed that the vote was rigged, and the desired result—a 90% vote for Nkrumah—was obtained. Referenda have also been used by President Marcos of the Philippines. In 1972, in 34,000 villages and city districts, citizens 15 years old and above assembled to give their verdict on Marcos's handling of events and on his plans for the future. These assemblies were designed by the President to serve as 'a direct forum for consultation between the leadership and the people'. The desired results were obtained. Finally a 'referendum' was held in Greece on 29 July 1973, during the period of military rule. The people were asked at the vote to confirm the change from monarchy to a republic, and to endorse Mr Papadopoulos as President until 1981. Voting NO would neither have restored the monarchy or overthrown

Papadopoulos. 78% of the voters voted YES.

Thus in general a plebiscite is a device at which the voters are asked to endorse an already established policy from which there is no possibility of a return to the status quo ante. By contrast the referendum (as it is used in the American States and the Swiss cantons) is a device in which the voters are invited to arbitrate between equally available solutions.

Clearly the question at issue in the British referendum cannot be isolated from the wider political implications of the result for British politics. But it is a clear question, and the Government have said that they will take the result as binding on them. We will return to the British referendum after dealing with the use of referenda elsewhere.

2   The Recourse to Referenda

An understanding of much of the modern use of referenda hinges on the distinction between constitutional and ordinary law. As we pointed out in the last chapter, no such distinction exists in Britain. Parliament is sovereign in the making of all laws. But elsewhere the basic 'rules of the game' of the political system are enshrined in a written constitution. Constitutions deal with such questions as the electoral system, the powers of government and parliament, the role of the courts and the respective powers—in a federal system—of central and constituent governments. In some countries they may also specify basic rights and liberties. Such constitutional law is normally entrenched in some way against change. The constitution itself will then define the special procedures by which it can be amended, procedures which are generally more complex than those for making ordinary law.

In Britain the constitution is unwritten. Certain fundamentals of the British system (for example the rule that governments must submit themselves to re-election within five years of taking office) are 'constitutional' but, can be altered—as ordinary laws—by the normal simple majority. Elsewhere constitutions may be completely rigid, or they may be capable of being changed by special procedure. A device which is sometimes used for this purpose—to legitimize changes in the basic 'rules of the game'—is the referendum.

We will briefly review the experience of those countries—generally liberal democracies of 'the West' or Australasia—which use or have used referenda. In doing so we will leave Denmark and Norway to a later section where we deal particularly with the referenda in 1972, on Common Market membership.

In surveying the countries which use referenda, nowhere are they used more frequently—and as such an integral part of the political system—as in Switzerland, and in many of the American States. It should be stressed that referenda are used in America only at the state and local levels, not at the federal level. Both countries are federations (in which the constituent states or cantons have independent powers) and both have written constitutions. Both use the initiative as well as the orthodox referendum. An initiative is a device by which members of the public may draft proposed laws or constitutional amendments, (both in various American States, only constitutional amendments in Switzerland) and by securing a designated number of signatures may require that the proposal be submitted to the voters at a referendum.

Switzerland: After a growth in the use of forms of direct popular action in the cantons in the 1860s the referendum and initiative were adopted in the Constitution of 1874. Today the possibilities for direct intervention of the people in the political process are extensive. A few cantons have even preserved the tradition of *Lanclesgemeinde,* the annual assembly of all adult male citizens with supreme legislative authority.

Basic to the other forms of direct democracy in Switzerland is the constitutional referendum. At the federal level all proposed amendments to the Swiss constitution which are approved by the parliament *must* be submitted to a referendum. Between 1920 and 1967 there were 47 such amendments, 36 of which were accepted. There has been some tendency for these amendments to increase the power of the Federal Government.

Constitutional amendments need not be proposed by Parliament, however, for there is also provision for the constitutional initiative. If 50,000 citizens propose an amendment the proposal is put to the people at a referendum. (The parliament may react to an initiative by proposing an amendment of its own for public decision, obtaining the withdrawal of the original initiative by its sponsors). All such changes in the constitution (whether they derived from parliament or an initiative) must be approved simultaneously by a majority of those voting and by a majority of the cantons.

Whereas most constitutional amendments have been accepted by the people, recent experience has shown that it is extremely difficult to induce the electorate to accept a popular initiative. Since 1935, 26 initiatives to alter the federal constitution have been voted on, and only one has been accepted.

The requirement for double acceptance—by a majority of the total population and by a majority of cantons—has proved to be a major obstacle. In 1955, for example, a socialist initiative aimed at providing increased protection for tenants received a popular majority, but since this was derived from only seven cantons, the initiative was defeated. Also the expenses of an initiative campaign are high, and a party may only rarely be able to mount the necessary campaign. A recent initiative that caused considerable controversy was that launched by Dr James Schwarzenbach, a right wing National Councillor and Zurich industrialist. His constitutional initiative (having gathered its signatures) was opposed overwhelmingly by parliament, parties, interest groups, churches and elite opinion. The object of the initiative was to cut back the number of foreigners working in Switzerland by a third in four years. At the referendum the Schwarzenbach amendment was defeated—but only by 54% to 46% and the Government had to introduce stricter control of immigration.

As well as constitutional changes, ordinary laws can also be submitted to referenda, but they cannot be proposed by initiative. The only procedure for having a referendum on an ordinary law is that in which 30,000 citizens, or eight canton governments, demand that a law be subject to a referendum, and do so within 90 days of the law's publication. In such cases, only a simple majority of those voting is required to accept or reject the law.

Since there is no initiative, the legislative challenge is something of a negative weapon and has generally had a conservative and delaying tendency. It allows latent hostility to be made effective and it has been possible at times to mobilize opposition fairly easily, even if only a single party comes out against the law. Between 1920 and 1967, 40 laws were challenged, and 23 of them were rejected.

The referendum is even more highly developed on the cantonal (and communal) levels where there is also a finance referendum and a legislative initiative.

What, then, can one say in summing up the Swiss experience. Firstly that referenda are an integral part of Swiss political life. Switzerland is a state of only 6 million people but is divided by religious, economic and linguistic differences. Thus government is a form of permanent coalition, and the process of governing involves constant compromise as well as constant consultation with the major interests. Part of this process is the knowledge that any of the interests may resort to a referendum if left unsatisfied.

The negative impact of the referenda and the advantage given to groups of substantial financial means may outweigh the impulsion which can be given reform through use of the initiative. But the rights to both devices are deeply embedded in the political culture of the country.

United States: The United States Constitution specifies the powers of the central branches of government and establishes the division between the federal and the state governments. Unlike the Swiss Constitution the US federal Constitution makes no provision for national referenda. It is in many of the states that forms of direct democracy are widespread. In all the states the people vote on new state constitutions or constitutional amendments. Massachusetts was the first state so to provide, in 1788, and the other states followed suit.

Not until the closing years of the nineteenth century did any American state authorize the use of the initiative and referendum as regular instruments for the making of ordinary laws. South Dakota in 1898 was the first state to adopt the initiative and referendum for ordinary legislation, with 19 other states following by 1928. One of these was Oregon, where the new procedures were introduced in 1904 following a campaign by a local populist and newspaperman who had studied the Swiss experience of direct government.

These developments were part of the Progressive movement, which reached its peak in 1912 when Theodore

Roosevelt polled 27% of the vote as a Progressive at the Presidential Election. The movement was concerned with reform and social justice as well as with 'giving the Government back to the people'. The movement reflected popular impatience with state legislatures that were often seen as being controlled by special interests, and sometimes by corrupt bosses. The direct vote of the people was to purify state politics. Thus the introduction of not only the referendum and the initiative, but also the recall,* the direct primary and women suffrage.

What, then is the present provision for referenda and initiatives in the American States. Firstly, in all American States new state constitutions and constitutional amendments must be submitted to a referendum. In 18 states there is provision for constitutional amendment by initiative. If a sufficient number of signatures are gathered in support of the petition, the amendment is submitted to the majority vote of the electorate.

39 States make provision for referenda on state legislation. These can take three forms. Firstly, by a petition of the people, (supported by a designated number of signatures), with the intention of repealing existing legislation. Secondly, in 20 states the legislature may submit laws to the electorate. Thirdly in 21 states there is a state constitutional requirement that certain questions be submitted to the people. Frequent referenda are held under this provision on bond issues, to raise finance for particular public services. Some states have all three types of provision for state legislation referenda. Finally 21

---

* A recall is a device designed to enable the electorate, through a special election, to replace a public official before the normal expiration of his term. Some states still use the device; in Oregon if a petition demanding the dismissal of an elected officer obtains enough signatures, there must be a referendum on the matter. The procedure has not generally been used to dismiss members of state legislatures.

states have provision for some form of ordinary law-making by initiative. Again, there is a stipulated number of signatures and the proposed law may then be put to majority vote at a referendum.

In practice the petition is not often used but when it is it tends to be a conservative weapon, giving voters the opportunity to turn down increases in taxation as well as extentions in the power of government. The American state referendum is used for compulsory constitutional amendments more than for any other purpose. State constitutions are detailed, and amendments can cover any question of the machinery of government, as well as questions of pensions or tax exemptions for veterans and widows and increased taxes for new public services. Again, taxpayers' revolts are not uncommon.

Two areas of public policy on which there have been frequent referenda are open-housing, and education. In the 1960s a number of states passed laws prohibiting racial discrimination in public housing. Between 1963 and 1968 ten cities and the state of California conducted open housing referenda. All were initiated by opponents who utilized the referendum provisions of city charters or state constitutions in an effort to cancel open housing legislation. In some communities, the petition drive was launched by right-wing groups such as the John Birch Society. Their strategy was successful in invalidating or delaying such measures in states and communities. Secondly, referenda on school budgets, taxes and bond issues are also an accepted part of state and local community politics in the USA.

It should be pointed out that state-wide referenda are but a small proportion of the large number of city and local referenda held in many states. This form of direct democracy is, as in Switzerland, an integral part of political life in the states and reflects the generally high levels of political interest and participation in America compared to Europe. Although the overall impact of the referendum on state politics should not be exaggerated, it does provide a further check on already divided state governments.

Outside Switzerland, and the United States how widely are referenda used? Writing in 1911, Clifford Sharp was only to point to Australia (in addition to the USA and Switzerland) in examining the use of referenda abroad.

Australia: Like Switzerland and the USA, Australia is a federation. The separate Australian colonies had considerable independence in 1901 when they jointly founded the Commonwealth of Australia. A written Constitution gave specific listed powers to the federal, or Commonwealth Government; the rest were left to the states.

The Constitution provides for the use of the referendum only in changing the Constitution. In fact the people have shown a marked aversion to changing the federal Constitution. Although there have been 86 attempts to initiate constitutional amendments in the period 1901-1974, 54 of these lapsed or were defeated without being submitted to the voters. Of the remaining 32 attempts which were submitted to' referenda, only five were accepted and eventually incorporated in the Constitution. The three most important of these related to the assumption of state debts by the federal Government, financial agreements between the seven governments, and the extension of Federal social services.

The overwhelming majority of the amendments involved requests by the central government for increased Federal legislative powers. The general conclusion must be that Australians have been conservative in using the referenda to give central government more power; the general tendency towards more Federal powers owes more to factors other than constitutional change.

In practice, a proposal for a constitutional amendment must be government sponsored. As in Switzerland the Australian Constitution requires that if a proposal is to be formally approved by the voters in a referendum, it must win an overall majority and a majority of votes in a majority of states. Voting is compulsory, and the ballot paper carries only the title of the proposed law.

The resistance of the original constitution to attempts at change reflects the strong feeling for the rights of the states. The most recent referenda on proposed constitutional amendments were held on 8 December 1973, when a clear majority of NO votes came from all states to amendments aimed at giving the Federal Government powers to control prices and incomes.

Finally, it is interesting that where there is constitutional provision for referenda for changes in the constitution, referenda tend also to be used occasionally for other important issues. This has happened in Australia. Four such polls have been held—two on the attempted secession of states from the Commonwealth, and two (in 1916 and 1917) on conscription.

Republic of Ireland: Under the 1937 Constitution a Bill amending the Constitution must be submitted to an advisory referendum after passing both Houses of Parliament. (There is also—as yet unused—provision for referenda on Bills of 'national importance').

Six referenda have been held under the above provision: issues have included a proposed change in the electoral system, and (more recently) the special constitutional position of the Roman Catholic Church, granting the vote to 18 year olds and, in 1972, membership of the EEC.

In the referendum on membership of the EEC a YES vote was urged by both the Government and the main opposition party, Fine Gael. The anti-marketeers included the Labour Party, Sinn Fein and the trade unions. The poll was 70% and there were 1,041,890 votes for entry and only 211,891 votes against.

Italy: The popular referendum or plebiscite did not form as essential a part of the Italian Fascist pattern of government as it did of the National Socialist. At the end of the War, with the final defeat of Italian Fascism, there was considerable hostility to the Monarchy. King Victor Emmanuel III had closely associated the monarchy with the Fascist regime. Groups favouring the monarchy insisted that the decision—between monarchic and republican forms of government—should be taken by a national referendum. Victor Emmanuel III abdicated on the eve of the referendum in favour of his son, who was less associated with fascism. Parties were split—the Christian Democrats declared in favour of a republic but left its members free to vote either way. The referendum, on 2 June 1946, rejected the monarchy by a vote of 12,717,923 to 10,710,284.

The same elections produced a Constituent Assembly that drew up a Constitution for the Italian Republic. This went into effect on 1 January 1948. This Constitution provides for referenda on constitutional laws or amendments to the Constitution. These must be requested within three months of the publication of the laws or amendments by one-fifth of the members of either chamber or not less than 500,000 electors or five regional councils. In fact, since 1948, no referenda have been held under this provision.

The Constitution also provides for the possibility of repealing an ordinary law, totally or partially, by popular referendum. Specifically excluded from these provisions are tax, budget and amnesty legislation, and treaties. On the demand of one fifth of either House, five Regional Assemblies, or 500,000 electors, a referendum must be held. A simple majority of votes cast is all that is required for the offending text to be repealed. In addition there are several other restrictions on the use of referenda for the purpose of repealing laws.

In fact the first and only referendum under Article 75 was held in May 1974. The opponents of the 1970 Divorce Law had collected the 500,000 signatures required for the holding of a referendum to repeal it. The issue of divorce split the Christian Democrat party and re-opened old issues about Church-State relations. Few politicians wanted a referendum, fearing it would create a precedent and further reduce the effectiveness of parliamentary legislation. However, contrary to the general belief that referenda tend to favour conservative policies, the results of the referendum showed in a solid majority for keeping the divorce law.

Thus in Switzerland, Austria, the Irish Republic and Italy (as well as Denmark) provision is made in written constitutions for referenda on constitutional amendments, and sometimes ordinary laws. In other countries, referenda have been held on an ad hoc basis, on major issues and not necessarily on constitutional changes.

Sweden: Swedish democracy is essentially representative. The referendum procedure was introduced by a constitutional amendment, passed in 1922. This allows for the opinion, or advice of the people to be taken at a referendum. The referendum is not compulsory for any kind of question; it is purely consultative. If the Government wish to consult the people through a referendum they must enact a specific statute law to that effect.

Only three referenda have been held in Sweden, in 1922, 1955 and 1957. In 1922 a very narrow majority of voters were against the introduction of prohibition of intoxicating liquors. In 1955 in a 53% poll an overwhelming majority rejected the idea that right hand driving should be substituted for left hand driving in Sweden. In 1963 the Social Democratic Government (after agreeing with the opposition parties) reversed this decision without holding a referendum.

The third referendum, in 1957, was on three competing schemes for a national pensions scheme to re-inforce the basic benefits of old age pensions. The parties and the interest groups had reached deadlock on the issue and as a last resort the Government evoked a referendum.

Potentially it was the clearest opportunity for direct democracy. In fact the results were entirely indecisive and subject to contrary interpretation. Three schemes, each backed by particular parties, were offered to the voters. The results, in a 72% poll, were as follows:

Alternative	%
1	45.8
2	15.0
3	35.3
Blank	3.9

Supporters of alternative 1 claimed the result to be a mandate for their superannuation proposal while supporters of alternatives 2 and 3 claimed that superannuation, as against their voluntary proposals, had gained no mandate.

Here is an example of the limitations of referenda in resolving complex issues. Its use, however, was part of a protracted process of debate and compromise which did finally lead to a new government bill in 1958.

New Zealand: The political system of New Zealand is based on the principle of parliamentary sovereignty and there is no written constitution. Thus there are no constitutional amendments. However the Electoral Act of 1956 does provide that amendments to it be submitted to referenda. It can be amended either by a 75% majority of the House of Representatives or by a referendum.

In 1967 there was a referendum on a proposal to extend the parliamentary term provided for in the Act. 678,960 people voted for the existing 3 year maximum term, while there were 317,973 votes for a maximum term of 4 years. Thus no change was made. This has been the only referendum on the Electoral Act.

Occasional referenda have been held on the following issues: licensing hours, betting regulations, conscription and prohibition.

Belgium: Belgium has a rigid constitution and no provision for referenda. However one referendum was held, on the return of the monarchy in 1950.

As in Italy the monarchy had been to some extent discredited by the war. King Leopold III remained in Belgium during the wartime period of occupation and moved to Austria as the Allies began to retake the Continent. After the war there was considerable opposition to Leopold's return. Finally in 1950, a referendum was held on the return of Leopold, and 58% of the population voted in his favour. He abdicated in favour of his son in 1951.

France: Britain has generally been characterized as having a relatively homogeneous society, a society in which there have been few deep cleavages or differences on the basis of religion or region. It has not therefore over-distorted or simplified the society to have a broadly two-party system structured on the important division of class. (That this may be changing we will discuss later). In France, however, the divisions have been greater; a system based on parliamentary sovereignty—as in Britain—produced only temporary, weak governments. Such a system characterized France in the Third Republic

69

from the 1870s to the fall of France to the Germans in 1940. This period had been a reaction from the one-man plebiscitory rule of the preceding period. By 1940 the parties and legislature were discredited. Elections had resolved nothing and weak Governments had been formed and had fallen in quick succession. The Vichy period of collaboration government during the war further discredited the politicians.

Referenda were held in 1945 and 1946 as part of the process by which the Fourth Republic Constitution emerged. But government remained weak, and was in particular unable to resolve the crisis in Algeria, where French military authorities, with the approval of French settlers, took over control in May 1958 and refused to recognize the government of France. By this time Charles de Gaulle, who had led the Free French during the war but retired from politics in 1946, was the only national leader left with great popular credit. In June 1958 de Gaulle was granted full powers by the French Assembly.

A new Constitution (of the Fifth Republic) was drawn up and submitted to the people of France at a referendum on 28 September 1958. Under the new constitution, approved by 78% of the voters, the Presidency was strengthened and parliament weakened. Provision was twice made for referenda. Article 89 required constitutional amendments to be approved by Parliament, and then confirmed either by referendum, or by a three-fifths majority of the two legislative houses sitting together. In addition, Article 11 allowed the President on the proposal of the government to submit to a referendum any bill on 'the organization of the public authorities'.

In January 1961, under Article 11, the President launched a referendum to justify his decision to establish a provisional executive in Algeria. In effect he also asked for a personal vote of confidence—one which would give him a free hand in the negotiations to come. The YES vote was 75.3% of votes cast. In its effect it was part referendum and part plebiscite: it demonstrated that the electorate were not prepared to fight to keep Algeria French, and confirmed popular confidence in the President. De Gaulle used the device again in April 1962 to approve the Evian agreements with the Algerian nationalists.

The President, distrustful of parties and Deputies used these votes as a means of governing, and of increasing his authority. In a third referendum in September 1962 de Gaulle submitted a proposed constitutional amendment to the people, invoking Article 11 as authority. He ignored both Article 89 and the fact that Article 11 was not thought to apply to constitutional amendments. Disregarding the protests, de Gaulle pressed on, and the amendment, providing for direct election of the President, received 61.8% support.

This was government by plebiscite. De Gaulle seemed to see his powers as unlimited by the constitution, as long as he could get public approval at a referendum. In April 1969 the President used the device again, and for the last time. Again there were vestigial elements of the orthodox referendum—the questions at issue were proposals for regional reform, and reform of the Senate. But at the end of a campaign notable for its lack of excitement de Gaulle transformed the question at issue by threatening to resign if his proposals were rejected. The vote became a plebiscite, with de Gaulle assuming that the voters would rally to him as a guarantor of order. In fact, with a turnout of 80%, 10,908,855 Frenchmen voted YES (37.1 of the register), and 11,943,283 voted NO. De Gaulle resigned and was gone.

The referendum has been held once since de Gaulle's departure. President Pompidou decided to use the device in April 1972 in order to seek the views of the French

71

people on the enlargement of the European Community. Pompidou's main purpose, however, seemed to be to strengthen his Government's position in domestic politics. Future use of this plebiscitory device might have been deterred by the record abstention of 39% of the electorate. As we have seen the impact of the referendum seemed to be as great in British politics as in French.

3   The EEC Referenda: The Scandinavian Experience

Britain is not unique in holding a referendum on the EEC issue: Norway, Denmark and Ireland all held referenda on whether or not to join the Common Market in 1972, while in the same year President Pompidou sought popular support by the same device for his decision to agree to widening the original membership of the EEC which reversed the previous French policy established by General de Gaulle. In examining the British referendum it is useful to look also at the experience of other countries, particularly the case of Norway and Denmark.

Norway: Like Britain Norway has no constitutional provision which requires the government to have recourse to a general referendum of the people on any issue. Nevertheless five referenda have been called since the country gained full independence from Sweden in 1905. Two were held in that year on the dissolution of the union with Sweden and on whether to institute either a monarchical or a republican regime. In 1919 a referendum was called which resulted in the prohibition of alcohol and another in 1926 repealed the prohibition. The fifth, held in 1972, was resorted to in order to determine whether or not the country should join in full membership of the EEC.

Although both Britain and Norway fall into the general category of western democracy their political systems are widely different. First, and most obviously, Norway is physically very large but has a relatively small population of some four millions. This geographic and demographic imbalance largely accounts for the enduring tension which exists between the centre and the periphery. Over the past century this tension has manifested itself in various ways: it can be seen in the religious disputes over the organization of the State Lutheran church; another confrontation centred on the creation of a new national language; and there have been continuing clashes arising from the resistence of the predominantly rural provinces to what they regard as the attempts by the governing elites in Oslo to impose urban social values on their traditional way of life.

Given these deep and lasting conflicts—to which must be added the conventional left-right ideological split—it is not surprising that Norway spawns a relatively large number of political parties which, with an electoral system based upon proportional representation, have usually been able to secure a base in the Storting (parliament). Another feature of the political scene (which in the past tended to be overlooked because of the dominance of Labour as the governing party, the war years excepted, from 1935 to 1965) is the apparent ease and speed with which a new party can rise and an old one disappear.

As in other countries the question of Norwegian membership of the EEC cut across party lines. Left to its own inclinations Norway would not have made overtures to Brussels. When Britain and Denmark decided to apply to join in 1961 the Labour Government felt that it had little alternative but to follow suit or else risk reduced access to two of Norway's major export markets. Popular feeling was against joining the EEC and a heated political debate ensued, one result of which was an acceptance that the issue would have to be subjected to a referendum. The two subsequent French vetoes erased the topic from the political agenda until it came up again at the end of the decade.

In 1970 the government, by now a coalition of the four non-socialist parties, decided once more to negotiate with the EEC. With the exception of the Communists and the Socialist People's Party, the other parties including Labour—the largest single parliamentary party—were formally committed, with varying enthusiasm and some dissentients, to favouring entry to the Common Market so long as Britain and Denmark also joined.

During the course of negotiations the marketeers suffered two major setbacks. First, Per Borten, the prime minister and leader of the Centre (Agrarian) party, was lukewarm if not hostile to Norway's membership of the EEC and leaked details of the negotiations to a leader of the *Folkebevegelsen* (the People's Movement Against Norwegian Membership of the EEC), a powerful pressure group formed in 1969. This episode led to the downfall of the coalition in March 1971 and Labour formed a minority government under Trygue Bratteli. The new administration continued negotiating and announced a successful outcome in January 1972. However, the Minister for Fisheries resigned in protest because of dissatisfaction with the terms obtained for the fishing industry.

In the meantime opinion polls showed considerable and continuing hostility to the idea of full Norwegian membership of the EEC. The constitution required that the Treaty of Accession be endorsed by three-quarters of all members of the Storting. At the outset of negotiations in 1970 it was estimated that roughly 110 out of the total of 150 MPs would vote in favour of joining the EEC, almost the necessary majority for ratification. But the constitutional requirement became a rather academic matter in view of the all-party commitment to hold a referendum. The period of the referendum campaign lasted from January to September 1972.

The campaign was both more intensive and extensive than anything previously experienced in Norway. Prime minister Bratteli called for a 'YES' and later in August made it a vote of confidence in the Government. Despite allegations of undue pressure being exerted on delegates he received overwhelming support at the Labour Party convention and at that of the Federation of Trade Unions. At their convention the Conservatives voted almost unanimously in favour of entry, while the conventions of the Centre, Communist and Socialist People's parties voted unanimously against it. The Christian People's party voted against by a majority of about 30% as did the Liberals at their conference by a similar margin, after which so deep was the division felt to be that the Liberals decided not to participate as a party in the referendum campaign.

The final result of the referendum vote was that 53.5% of the electorate voted against Norway's full membership of the EEC and 46.5% voted in favour. The Labour government resigned and was succeeded by a small, weak three-party coalition of Liberals, and the Centre and Christian People's parties whose main task as a caretaker government was to arrange a free trade pact with the EEC.

The pro-market case had had the support of a large majority of parliamentarians, the Conservatives and the Labour Party (excluding a left-wing minority), most of the press and the representative organizations of business and the trade unions. Yet despite this impressive backing the majority of Norwegians voted 'NO'. Electoral results from the referendum show that opposition to joining the Common Market included the vast majority of rural voters, particularly the farmers and fisherfolk, for whom Oslo had always seemed too remote, let alone Brussels. Additional data from opinion polls reveals that disaffected urban radicals also opposed the Market as did a very high proportion of young voters—those under thirty —including the young Conservatives whose elders proved to be among the staunchest pro-marketeers.

In many ways the results of the referendum were evocative of the pattern of Norwegian politics in the period from the later nineteenth century until the Labour party's rise to power in the mid-1930s. The enduring centre-periphery cleavage traditionally based on the issues of religion, temperance and language now also embraced the EEC question. This meant that the Labour party was unable to mobilize its full grass roots support for the Common Market cause, and after the referendum its more left-wing members who had opposed the official party line left to form their own party which, in turn, has recently merged with the Communists to form the new Socialist Left party. This defection, however, did not prevent the Labour party from emerging as the largest single party in the 1973 General Election, after which it again formed the government, although its share of the poll dropped by 11%. The Liberals, too, lost much of their previous support during the referendum and were all but anihilated in the General Election. Though its membership was very divided over the referendum the Christian People's party nevertheless managed to increase their representation in the Storting at the Election.

Why the referendum resulted as it did has been the subject of much speculation: why, unlike Ireland and Denmark, did Norway reject full membership of the EEC and why, in the process, did it break with the pragmatic, consensus approach to decision-making which hitherto had been regarded as the hallmark of post-war politics throughout Scandinavia?

A number of possible explanations have been given. First, it is a relatively new nation and, like Ireland, achieved full national independence only in this century;

76

and furthermore, like Denmark, it suffered five years of German occupation during the war. Thus it is jealous of its national sovereignty.

Secondly, it is geographically remote from the heartland of Europe and its main supra-national orientation is Nordic rather than continental. Thirdly, it is much less dependent on the British market than either Denmark or Ireland.

Fourthly, it has been suggested, that the referendum with its straight YES/NO choice was a bewildering experience for Norwegian voters who are used to a variety of choices as a result of the multi-party system and proportional representation. The situation was further exacerbated by the strange political alliances which the campaign produced whereby the Conservative and Labour parties, traditionally antagonistic, joined with their respective supporters in business and the unions in support for EEC membership. These factors are said to have 'cross-pressured' people in making up their minds, which accounts for the high proportion of voters usually loyal to Labour going against the official party policy.

Fifthly, the fact that the party system was unable by itself to deal with the question of Norway's EEC membership and had to refer the decision to the electorate by means of a referendum led inevitably, as in Britain, to the parties playing a more muted role than is customary in electioneering. Their traditional campaigning functions were largely taken over by the strong *ad hoc* organizations of supporters and opponents of the EEC. The *Folkebevegelsen,* the main anti-market pressure group, secured a head start at the opening of negotiations in 1970. In contrast, the pro-marketeers were inhibited from fully pressing their cause until after the exact terms were known in January 1972. The opponents concentrated on the political issues of the loss of national sovereignty and self-determination which resonated favourably among the

77

independent-minded voters in the rural areas. It also attracted the urban radicals and the younger generation who saw the EEC as a group of capitalistic, privileged nations united in maintaining their comparative advantage *vis-a-vis* the third world. A growing awareness of the ecological implications in the pursuit of economic growth, to which the EEC was felt to be insufficiently sensitive, provided a further plank in the opponents' platform. The advocates of EEC membership, reluctant to emphasize the possible political advantages, concentrated their arguments on the economic benefits which might accrue to Norway.

Dramatic though the referendum episode was in the modern history of Norway it is difficult to say whether the EEC issue was the prime cause of the political upheaval which surrounded it or whether it simply acted as a catalyst, accentuating and hastening developments which were already under way. It is a question which can and, in due course, indubitably will be asked about the domestic political context of Britain's relations with the EEC.

In Norway, as in Britain, the decade prior to the referendum had been characterized by an increased volatility amongst the electorate, one effect of which in 1965 had been the ending of thirty years of Labour rule. A 'generation gap' was emerging together with a greater demand for popular participation in decision-making which played some part in deciding to hold a referendum. All of these factors, as in Britain, served to weaken the existing party system: new ideas and new forms arose to challenge existing arrangements and procedures and their growth was accelerated by the EEC question.

Denmark: In Denmark the referendum was not part of the constitution until 1953, when, on giving up the upper house, Conservatives insisted on provision for referenda as a check on the lower chamber. (The only referendum

78

held before 1953 was in 1916 approving the Government's decision to transfer the Danish West Indies to the USA).

Under the Constitution, constitutional amendments are subject to referendum. In addition, and also under the Constitution, Bills passed by the Parliament (The Folketing) may be put to a referendum at the request of one-third of its members. Bills on finance or taxation, or Bills introduced for the purpose of discharging existing Treaty obligations, are exempt.

Any action which involves the transfer of power from the government to an international body, such as would follow from membership of the EEC, is subject to a special ratification procedure under the Danish Constitution of 1953. The constitution requires either that the necessary legislation be passed by a five-sixths majority in the Folketing or, if it receives no more than a simple majority, it must be endorsed subsequently in a popular referendum; the bill will only fall if it is rejected by a majority equivalent to at least thirty per cent of the total electorate.

Seven referenda have been held since 1953. Four of these have been on the voting age in Danish elections. The 1953 Constitution provided for a referendum on whether the voting age should be 23 or 21; it also provided that future changes in the voting age could only be made if the amendment was subjected to popular referendum. Referenda in 1953 and 1961 decided that the voting age should be 23 and 21 respectively. After the parties failed to agree, a referendum on 24 June 1969 substantially rejected a proposal to reduce the voting age to 18. In September 1971 the voting age was reduced to 20 following a referendum.

Until 1971 the question of Denmark's membership of the EEC was hardly a matter of political dispute—at least in the Folketing. From 1961 to 1971 more than the necessary five-sixths of all MPs favoured entry and it was only after the general election of September 1971 that enough oponents were returned to activate the referendum clause in the constitution. However, in the previous May the Folketing had voted to submit the bill accepting membership of the EEC to a referendum even if it had been passed by the five-sixths majority.

Like Ireland and Norway, Denmark would not have unilaterally initiated steps to enter the EEC. As in the case of the other two countries it opened negotiations along with Britain and Britain's entry was a stated condition of Denmark's entry. The main reason for this was the overwhelming importance of the British market for Danish exports, particularly its agricultural products which in 1958 accounted for almost a half of all exports. After Britain, West Germany was the next most important market for Danish agriculture, which was an additional reason for seeking to join the EEC. By 1971 agriculture's share of the export trade had dropped to 21 per cent which in one way decreased Denmark's dependence on its traditional markets. In another way, however, the rapid development of its industry required easy access to a large market of the kind afforded by the EEC, so that the profound structural changes which had occurred in the economy were largely self-cancelling in regard to Denmark's relationship with the Common Market. The failure to form a Nordic economic union which had been seriously mooted between 1968 and 1970 gave an added ground for proceeding with negotiations to join the EEC.

The pro-market lobby consisted of the four main parties, *viz* the Social Democrats, the Radical Liberals, the Conservatives and the Agrarian Liberals, together with the central organizations representing the trade unions and business and the majority of the press. The pattern, with two exceptions, was not too dissimilar from that obtaining in Norway: the exceptions were the

Liberals and the farmers, both of whom supported entry. The pro-EEC campaign was orchestrated by the Committee for Danish Affiliation with the European Communities.

The anti-marketeers comprised the Socialist People's party and other left-wing groups, a minority of Social Democrats and Radical Liberals, some trade unions including the powerful General Workers and Metal Workers, and a few newspapers. Most of the opposition groups united under the banner of the People's Movement Against the European Communities, but the dissident Social Democrats formed their own separate pressure group.

After a good deal of bargaining between the Danish and Norwegian Governments over the timing of their respective referenda Denmark agreed to hold its poll a week later on 2 October 1972. Reference has already been made to some of the similarities and differences between the two countries over the EEC issue, but there are other important points of comparison which deserve mention.

As in Norway, a non-socialist coalition began the Danish negotiations in 1970 but was succeeded by a minority Social Democratic government in 1971 which had to complete the negotiations. Another common feature was that the Social Democrats, like the Norwegian Labour Party, had a small but not insignificant minority of opponents to the EEC in its parliamentary ranks. The governing party was not helped by the fact that for the first six months of 1971 the opinion polls registered growing opposition to EEC membership. During the whole of the previous decade anti-market sentiment had never risen above 10 per cent, while pro-market feeling was usually recorded at between 50% and 60%. In the first half of 1971, however, opposition to the EEC rose to 30% while support for it dropped to just under 40%. In the event support later picked up and the result of the referendum was that 63.5% of the electorate voted for Danish membership and 36.5% voted against; the negative vote in Norway the previous week had no apparent effect.

The Social Democrats, like their Norwegian counterparts, did not manage to mobilize all their supporters to vote for entry to the EEC; a large minority of traditional Social Democrat voters opposed Danish membership. Perhaps the most striking difference between the results of the two referenda was that whereas Oslo and its environs polled a pro-market majority as against an anti-market majority in the Norwegian provinces, in Denmark the reverse happened: Copenhagen and its suburbs voted a slight majority against the market while the rest of the country voted overwhelmingly the other way.

Comparisons Between Britain and Scandinavia: Britain, Denmark and Norway are very different from one another in regard to their political cultures and their systems of government. It is sometimes possible to draw historical comparisons about a particular event as we have briefly attempted above in the case of the two Scandinavian nations, but it is altogether a more hazardous undertaking to predict, on the basis of the Danish and Norwegian experiences, the course of the last stages and the final outcome of the British Referendum.

It is clear, however, that Scandinavian experience has already influenced the British approach. It is obvious, for example, that Harold Wilson has been anxious to minimize internal dissent within the Labour Party by having a much shorter campaign than was the case in the other two countries. He has also endeavoured to avoid the mistake of the Norwegian Labour Prime Minister by making the Referendum a vote of confidence in the Government: by suspending, or modifying, collective cabinet responsibility on the issue he hopes to be able to re-unite the Labour party more easily whatever the result. Similarly, the refusal to allow the declaration of results on a constituency basis will obscure the distribution of votes sufficiently so that local differences will be less obvious than was the case in Norway.

It is apparent, too, that the pro-market lobby in Britain is anxious to secure a high poll in the referendum. In Norway a lower than usual turnout resulted in a 'NO' vote, whereas in Denmark, and Ireland for that matter, unprecedently high turnouts resulted in very large 'YES' majorities.

Perhaps, in the end, the major difference between the British Referendum and those of other countries on the Common Market issue is that it is taking place three years later in a world that is very different. Since the Irish and Scandinavian referenda the oil crisis has occurred, which, despite the prospect of North Sea oil, hit Britain and the rest of Western Europe very hard and has possibly assisted in promoting a greater sense of European identity among the British people. Secondly, the intervening years have seen the position of the United States of America weakened by internal political scandals, and by a series of military and diplomatic defeats resulting in Communist victories in South-East Asia; its NATO allies in Europe may sense that their super-power partner may be beginning to move towards a more withdrawn and isolationist posture in world affairs, reluctant to defend anywhere beyond its own continent. The actions of the oil producers and the changed position of America may well influence a majority of British electors to vote in favour of remaining in the EEC as the only defence against external events.

Another major difference between the British vote and the other countries is that the electorate has to vote on whether or not Britain should *remain* in the EEC, whereas in the other three countries their citizens were invited to decide on whether to *join* the EEC or not. Since 1972 the record of the EEC has not been particularly dynamic or spectacular. Its Commission has lost ground as a result of the institution of regular summit meetings of heads of government which now take all the major decisions, and little has happened to threaten the position of national governments within the EEC. For their part Ireland and Denmark have already stated they will not leave the EEC should Britain decide to relinquish membership.

4 Conclusions

The use of the Referendum, as we have defined it, is largely restricted to a small number of the 'liberal democracies' of Australasia, North America, Western Europe and Scandinavia.

Even where the referendum is used it is generally used only occasionally. Only in Switzerland and in some of the American States are referenda accepted as part of the day to day political process. Australia, with its 36 referenda in the period 1901-1974 is also unusual in its relatively frequent use of the device for attempted constitutional changes. Among the other countries surveyed the number of referenda held in this century has tended to vary from one to eight.

Provision for the initiative is especially limited: it is used only in Switzerland, various American states and Australia. In each country initiatives have rarely resulted in constitutional change. Similarly only in a few countries (Switzerland, Italy, some American States) is there provision for the challenge of ordinary laws by petition (followed by referenda).

Generally there is either constitutional provision for obligatory referenda on constitutional changes (Switzerland, Australia, Irish Republic and Italy) or the Government have chosen on an ad hoc basis to hold referenda on particular issues. In federations referenda have tended to be held on attempts to increase federal as against state or canton powers. But countries with and without written constitutions have held referenda on 'constitutional' questions such as the monarchy (Belgium, Italy and Norway), and changes in electoral or parliamentary procedures (Ireland and New Zealand).

Not all issues on which referenda have been held have been of major importance. A number have been held on what in Britain would be regarded as free-vote issues, indicating that they are not part of normal party politics. Obvious examples have been conscription, left hand driving and licensing and betting regulations. Others have considerable constitutional overtones—Church-State relations, divorce, voting ages and prohibition.

The results of referenda on these questions about the rules of the game, or about issues on which the parties have no strong view, are generally accepted by Governments. On major questions, turnout has been high. In these circumstances it is difficult for any government not to accept the popular verdict. A referendum can provide a policy or a decision with a unique form of legitimacy.

Britain compares with the Scandinavian and Western European countries which have used referenda in being a traditionally more homogeneous society. Thus issues which elsewhere have been sufficiently important to groups in the community (religious groups, for example) to warrant a referendum in order to get public consent for a policy, have been settled in Britain without much opposition. An example might be the case of the 'agreed syllabus' providing for religious instruction in the British 1944 Education Act.

Further, as we mentioned earlier, the constitution is long established. The monarchy has not been an issue. There is no federal division of powers. If, as we shall argue later, there are pressures to define and codify the British 'constitution' (whether because of demands for a bill of rights, substantial federal provisions involved in a devolution settlement or perhaps an erosion of the two party system) then this could lead to discussion of referenda as a possible means of validating future changes.

Generally, however issues have been settled through the party system. Elections have produced Governments. In a number of the countries where occasional referenda have been held there has been no means through the electoral system of giving a clear mandate to a government. Where the number of parties is large, reflecting religious, regional, racial and linguistic differences, elections produce no clear majority. Instead they produce politicians, who then bargain in order to produce coalition governments. In these countries, some basic problems cannot be solved by this compromise process, and a mandate is needed. Thus the only way of providing this mandate is by putting the question directly to the electors.

This is a tentative suggestion. Clearly it does not apply to New Zealand or Australia, and there are divided societies where referenda are not used. But in Italy, Belgium and the Scandinavian countries, as well as Switzerland, this does seem to be a factor. In the Republic of Ireland the fact that the two dominant parties are similar in interest and ideology may also partly explain the use of referenda when a specific public decision is required.

Although several referenda have had great impact—those in France in 1946 and 1969 and those over the monarchies, for example—the extent of the use of referenda should not be exaggerated. They are of severely limited use (as the Swedish case indicates) in dealing with the most insoluble economic and social problems of modern government.

4 The Campaign: Interests and Issues

1 The 'Rules of the Game'

One of the direct ways in which the Government has taken note of the Norwegian experience in organizing the Referendum is in its decision to limit the duration of the campaign. The date of the vote, originally scheduled for the third week in June, was brought forward to 5 June. On that date the form of the ballot paper as laid down as a schedule to the Referendum Bill will be as follows:

> The Government have announced the results of the renegotiation of the United Kingdom's terms of membership of the European Community.
>
> DO YOU THINK THAT THE UNITED KINGDOM SHOULD STAY IN THE EUROPEAN COMMUNITY (THE COMMON MARKET)?
>
> YES
>
> NO

There has been some criticism from the opinion poll organizations that the Government should have consulted them in drawing up the question. Dr Henry Durant (in a letter to the *Times*, 23 April) has argued that both alternatives should be specified in the question. Thus his suggested question would read:

> Do you think that the United Kingdom should stay in or get out of the Common Market?

The voter's cross, he suggests, would be placed against 'stay in' or 'get out'.

This consideration is a crucial one in opinion polling

but in the case of a national referendum, where the real alternative is highly publicized, the lack of a specified alternative in the question seems unlikely to have much effect on the result.

A second question of organization and procedure is that of who is eligible to vote? The Referendum Act provides that the electorate should include those who were on the current Parliamentary register (which came into force in February 1975) together with Peers (who are not eligible to vote in Parliamentary elections). In addition there are to be special arrangements made enabling members of the Armed Services and their wives who are eligible for registration as service voters to vote in the Referendum whether or not they are so registered. Voting will be conducted by the service units.

Other than this the facilities available for postal and proxy voting will also apply to the referendum poll. Postal votes, as at Parliamentary elections, may be claimed by those who are unable to vote in person because of the nature of their employment, blindness or physical incapacity, having to make a journey by air or sea or because they no longer live at the qualifying address.

All civilians overseas who are registered will be able to vote by proxy but, despite pressure from other parties, the Government have said that it is impossible either to make provision for overseas civilians to vote overseas or for those overseas who are not registered to register specially for the Referendum poll. Such provision, the Government argued, would be too complex to organize in the time available and would involve loopholes which would lead to abuse.

A third question of organization relates to the procedure for the count. Here the Government have reversed their original intention under considerable backbench pressure. In the White Paper and the Bill provision was made for all the votes to be counted

88

centrally in London (at Earls Court). But on 24 April the Government bowed to demands from all parties and announced that the votes on 5 June would be counted on a county basis (and on a regional basis in Scotland). The announcement followed the carrying on a free vote of a Labour backbench amendment to the Bill providing for county and regional declarations. A Liberal amendment calling on the count and declaration to be conducted on a constituency basis was defeated. The change was something of a victory for backbenchers of all parties and for Parliament as a whole. There are only three constituencies, Orkney and Shetland, the Western Isles and the Isle of Wight which are co-terminous with the electoral districts for the poll. Otherwise counting on a county and regional basis is an entirely new departure.

A further point is the provision for the size of the poll and majority. There is no specification of a minimum turn out (in order that the poll be valid) and the provision is that the result rests on a simple majority—without qualifications or conditions. An amendment to provide that the Referendum vote would be null and void if the overall vote was less than 60% and if there was not a two-thirds overall majority one way or the other was rejected by a majority of 89.

The Government have provided a number of general rules for the campaign itself. Two 'umbrella' organizations are officially recognized in the Act: Britain in Europe (promoting a YES vote) and the National Referendum Campaign (promoting a NO vote). The Act further provides that a grant not exceeding £125,000 be provided towards the expenses incurred by them or by organizations affiliated to them for the purposes of the Referendum. The two organizations are required to keep accounts for the period of the campaign.

The Government is also to distribute to each household a popular version of the White Paper on renegotiation, an account of how the Referendum is to be conducted and a single document containing statements of between 1,000 and 2,000 words on each of the opposing views, together with answers given to each side to the same sets of questions.

Lastly, the Government have pledged themselves to be bound by the verdict of the British people as expressed in the Referendum result.

2 The Agreement to Differ

For only the second time in recent British political history a Government of the day has officially suspended collective cabinet responsibility and allowed cabinet ministers to differ in public on a particular policy. The first occasion was in November 1931 following the Election, with an enormous Parliamentary majority, of a National Government with a 'doctor's mandate' to deal with the economic crisis. Ramsay MacDonald was Prime Minister and the Government contained both Conservatives and most Liberals. The division came over protection which most Conservatives supported but which the orthodox Liberals, led by Sir Herbert Samuel, strongly opposed. Since the leading Minister, Philip Snowden, was also a free trader, the Government—only in office a few weeks—dared not provoke a split in the coalition in which Snowden and the orthodox Liberals would resign. Thus the cabinet agreed on the device of the agreement to differ. Sir Herbert Samuel and Isaac Foot, both dissident Liberal Ministers, made powerful speeches in favour of free trade under the agreement. The Liberals remained in the Government on this basis until they resigned over the Ottawa agreement on imperial preference in 1932.

The situation is now rather different. Following the Dublin summit, the climax of the process of re-negotiation, Mr Wilson let it be known that he intended to recommend to the cabinet that they accept the new terms and themselves recommend that Britain remain in the Common Market. On 19 March 1975 the cabinet decided by a 16-7 vote to formally recommend that Britain stay in the EEC. The seven dissident ministers were Michael Foot (Employment), Tony Benn (Industry), Peter Shore (Trade), Barbara Castle (Social Services), John Silkin (Planning and Local Government), Eric Varley (Energy) and William Ross (Scotland).

Harold Wilson announced on 8 April that dissident ministers were to be allowed to speak against the cabinet's majority recommendation during the campaign but no minister was to oppose the cabinet's decision in the House of Commons, even from the backbenches. On 10 April Eric Heffer, Minister of State at the Department of Industry, became the first victim of the ruling when he was dismissed for flouting it. He spoke in the Commons against the cabinet's EEC recommendation.

The Prime Minister has also argued that ministers and Labour MPs should not dispute with each other in public. Further, following an attempt by the NEC to pass a motion committing the party to campaign against the government's recommendation, Wilson wrote letters to the anti-Market ministers on the NEC in which he stated that they were free to campaign against the cabinet recommendation but not to organize opposition to the Government. They were not to oppose Government policy in the NEC.

By such means has the Prime Minister attempted to contain the division in his Government. What remains to be seen in the rest of the campaign is whether he can contain the division between anti- and pro-marketeers in the party as a whole. An early attempt by Ian Mikardo and the NEC to commit the Party machine fully to the anti-Market cause (on 26 March) was not successful, but following the Labour Party conference on 26 April the

NEC arranged a special meeting for the 30th with the apparent intention of getting the full weight of Labour's headquarters machine thrown into the campaign against EEC membership.

It is interesting that only the Labour Party decided to hold a special conference on the issue unlike Norway where all the Parties held special conferences on the issue. The conference voted against Britain's continued membership of the Common Market by 3,724,000 votes to 1,986,000—slightly less than two to one. It is disputed whether this gives the Party the right to campaign nationally for a NO vote. Shirley Williams has argued that a two-thirds majority at conference is necessary before a proposal can become Party policy. This question remains to be resolved. The anti-Marketeers may feel, given the opinion polls in March and April, that only a large national Labour Party campaign can now have some impact. On the other hand, there may be many constituency parties who will take a neutral position in the campaign, either because their MP and their constituency party disagree, or because there are divisions within their constituency party. That this may be so may be indicated by the fact that according to the *Times* (28 April) only 452 of the 630 constituency parties sent delegates.

It is likely that Transport House will make campaign literature available but any proposal for a costly national campaign by the Labour Party against the Market is likely to be strongly resisted.

3   The Opposing Forces

The Parties: The Prime Minister enters the crucial weeks of the campaign with a majority of the Parliamentary Labour Party lined up against him. In the debate on 9 April the Government motion approving the recommendation of the Government was carried—on a free vote—by 396 votes to 170. But of the 315 Labour MPs

145 voted against the motion and only 137 voted in favour. Full figures for the Labour Party vote (including tellers) were presented in the *Guardian* (11 April):

	For	Against	Did not vote
Cabinet	14	7	0
Junior Ministers	31	31	9
Backbench	92	107	24
Total	137	145	33

Labour Party Vote. Motion on European Community (Membership) 9 April 1975.

It is significant that of the 85 Labour MPs who had entered the House since 1971, 49 voted against the Market and 26 in favour. (10 did not vote.) They contrast with the generally pro-Market Labour Party MPs who first entered the House in the 1964 and 1966 Elections. Although by no means all the anti-Marketeers were on the Left, virtually all the Left were against the Market; of the 69 members of the Tribune group in Autumn 1974, 57 of them voted against the Market on 10 April 1975. It is also generally true that the MPs who have recently entered Parliament (in the 1974 Elections) have been more to the left of the Party.

Moving from the Parliamentary Party to the Party in the country, we have already noted the 2:1 vote against the Market of the special Party Conference. The National Executive Committee is strongly anti-Market. This has been reflected in its attempts to involve the party machine in a Labour Party campaign against the Market. The NEC is also to the fore in promoting the adoption of more socialist measures by the Party. Since 1970 there is real truth in the argument that the division in the Party reflects the wider division between what have been called 'social democrats' and 'socialists'. Although ministers like Eric Varley and William Ross and backbenchers such

93

as Douglas Jay, Sir Arthur Irvine and Sir A. Irvine are generally anti-Market, those who have felt most strongly about the issue have been on the Left.

The Conservative Party now stands overwhelmingly for a YES vote on 5 June. In the vote on the Government motion on 10 April, 249 Conservative MPs voted for the motion, 18 did not vote and only 8 voted against. This represents a considerable dissipation of Conservative anti-Market support since October 1971 when 39 Conservatives voted against the principle of entry. The Conservative MPs on record against the Market in April 1975 include Neil Marten, Roger Moate, John Biffen and Richard Body. There may be several reasons for the fall in Conservative anti-Market feeling. Some may see the issue as already settled, some may argue that Treaties, however repugnant, should not be abrogated, while others may find the idea of allying with the Labour Left distasteful and fear the wider implications of a NO vote.

In the 10 April vote the Liberals voted 12:0 in favour of the Market (one Liberal did not vote). There are both Conservative and Liberal campaign organizations against the Market but these are weak compared with the general pro-Market support of the two Parties. There are in fact two Conservative anti-Market groups, Conservatives against the Market and Conservatives against the Treaty of Rome (CATOR). CATOR has claimed (*Guardian* 15 March) that 82% of constituency parties replying to their letter have stated that their association will either be taking no part in the campaign or will be preserving a balance by presenting both sides of the argument. Although the Conservative Central Office may play a considerable role, at the constituency level opinion may well be more divided.

All 13 Plaid Cymru and SNP MPs voted against the Market. 6 Ulster Unionists voted against the Market (including their leader James Molyneaux and Enoch

94

Powell) while four others did not vote. The Communist Party are against the Market although there is a small unofficial Communists for Europe Group. The National Front is also strongly opposed but has been denied affiliation to the official anti-Market organization.

The interests: It is too early in the campaign to fully classify all the interest groups or to gauge their impact in the campaign. On 28 April the Confederation of British Industry launched a £50,000 campaign for Britain remaining in the Market. On the 20 March leaders of the National Farmers Union voted overwhelmingly in favour of membership. Only two of the 118 country representatives who attended a special debate voted against, with five abstaining.

The Trades Union Congress has officially come out in opposition and so have most of the large Unions. Nevertheless an analysis of the trade union voting at the special Party Conference suggests a narrower margin of anti-Market Party voting than in the past. Union voting on 26 April together with size of bloc votes were as follows:

Against EEC		*For EEC*	
Total: 3,724,000 including:		Total: 1,986,000 including:	
Transport Workers	1 m.	General and Municipal	650,000
Engineers	980,000	Electricians & Plumbers	350,000
Miners	264,000	Shopworkers	293,000
ASTMS	151,000	Post Office Workers	183,000
Public Employees	150,000	Railwaymen	164,000
Agricultural Workers	75,000	APEX (clerical workers)	100,000
Boilermakers	71,000	Iron & Steel trades	94,000
Post Office Engineers	61,000		
Tailors & Garment	62,000		
Transport Salaried Staffs	60,000		

The TGWU and ASTMS are particularly active in the anti-Market campaign. In reply to the predominantly anti-Market impact a Trade Union Alliance for Europe is to be launched on 1 May. Finally on the anti-EEC side of the campaign is the National Union of Students.

The 'umbrella' groups: Of the two 'umbrella' groups Britain in Europe has been the more prominent. Prominent members include Sir Con O'Neill, William Whitelaw, Roy Jenkins, Cledwyn Hughes, Reginald Maudling and Jo Grimond. On the anti-Market side the National Referendum Campaign, the official 'umbrella' group for those proposing a NO vote, has been more of a formal than an active body. Its Chairman is Neil Marten. On the anti-Market side much of the running has been made by Tribune rallies at which some of the dissident ministers, Michael Foot, Peter Shore, Tony Benn, and Barbara Castle, have been prominent. Clive Jenkins is one trade unionist who has been quite willing to share platforms with Conservatives such as Richard Body and Neil Marten and with Enoch Powell.

4 The Debate

Again, we can only discuss the trends up to the final five weeks of the campaign. We deal with some of the economic issues in chapter 5.

One issue, which may increase in importance as the campaign continues concerns not the Common Market itself but the implications of a 'NO' vote. Towards 5 June some may well try to suggest a Gaullist picture of anarchy and chaos following such a result. William Whitelaw has suggested that there might be a constitutional crisis if the vote was 'NO'. The Conservative Party has—unlike the Government—not committed itself to accepting the result of the Referendum, especially if the poll is small or inconclusive. In addition the leader of the Liberal Party has suggested that Liberal Members in the House of Commons would vote in favour of Britain's staying in the European Community, even if the Referendum goes against continued British membership. Thus, if there was a 'NO' vote, especially on a low poll, there could be considerable difficulties for a Labour Government attempting to pass any legislation necessary to withdraw Britain from the EEC. It is by no means clear that some of the more prominent Labour pro-Marketeers would accept a 'NO' vote: in contrast, the most prominent anti-Market ministers have said that they would accept the result of the vote.

Despite these difficulties the leading anti-Market ministers have published a timetable providing for British withdrawal from the EEC by 1 January 1976. In an earlier statement on 23 March the same ministers stressed that to them the gravest disadvantages of membership were political. They argued that the rights of the British people and the power of Parliament remained subordinate to the non-elected Commission and the Council of Ministers in Brussels. The 'debate' so far has tended to be concerned with a central point made by the anti-Market ministers—that the 'power of future British governments to influence the economy in the interest of the British people has been gravely weakened.' Tony Benn warned workers and employers in the West Midlands that the chances of receiving Government aid for ailing industries would be gravely damaged if Britain stayed in the Common Market. Other anti-Marketeers have also stressed the powers of the Commission to interfere with British policies, especially in the area of greater public ownership. Much of the debate has been conducted on these issues, with pro-Marketeers defensively replying to such attacks and stressing that ultimately the Commission, like the Pope, has few divisions.

In the debate so far we have heard little of the self-confident Europeanism of earlier stages of the British discussion on the EEC. This may in part reflect the feeling of pro-Marketeers that it is up to the anti-Marketeers to make the case for coming out, not for them to establish the case for entering the EEC. Nevertheless, it is difficult not to get the impression that some of the great hopes for the Market have faded and that the case for continuing membership is now more often put negatively—in terms of the economic costs of withdrawal and isolation. Michael Foot made a strong attack on this case in his speech at the Party conference:

> Don't be afraid of those who tell us we cannot run our affairs, that we haven't the ingenuity to mobilize our resources and overcome our economic problems.

If the positive case for membership has been muted, though, some of the arguments of the anti-Market ministers have seemed to exaggerate—even to such a fellow opponent of entry as Eric Heffer—the control of the European Commission over domestic policy. Heffer, in a television interview on 26 April, felt that the power of the Commission over normal British policy making had been overemphasized.

The arguments of what might loosely be called the 'Tribune' ministers have concentrated on the incompatibility of the policies they foresee for Britain and the free market competitive economy that is the basis of the Treaty of Rome. The emphasis has been on 'socialism in one country'. In contrast free traders such as Douglas Jay oppose the whole idea of a trade bloc which inhibits British freedom to buy the cheapest food and materials from any country. The Conservative Neil Marten also bases his case on the ability of the British people freely to rule themselves. Right and Left are thus agreed on the importance of national sovereignty on the main issue. As on the issue of the House of Lords, Michael Foot and Enoch Powell have allied in defence of British Parliamentary sovereignty.

5 Scottish and Welsh Nationalism

There are several reasons for discussing Wales and Scotland separately in relation to the Referendum. Firstly the way Scottish and Welsh people vote may be crucial in the poll. Secondly, the growth of 'nationalism' and of demands for self-government lead to the increasing possibility of some form of federal structure for the United Kingdom. If this happened the division of power would presumably be defined in a written constitution, and the Referendum might be considered as a means of changing this constitution in the future. Thirdly, as a constitutional question, there could well be demands for a referendum on the issue of Welsh and Scottish devolution or independence.

The strategy of the present Scottish National Party dates back to the Scots National League, which rejected the notion that anyone could achieve independence through parties which were essentially and insurmountably Unionist. Various amalgamations of the League and other groups led to the emergence of the Scottish National Party in 1934. The present strength of the Party, however, dates from its by-election successes in the 1960s. The General Election in February 1974 resulted in the return of seven SNP MPs. In October 1974 the SNP won 11 seats and gained 30% of the vote making them the second Party in Scotland in terms of popular vote.

The Welsh Nationalist Party, Plaid Cymru, was founded in 1925 but only received its first electoral encouragement in two by-elections in 1945 when its candidates each obtained over 6,000 votes. It was not until the 1966 Carmarthenshire by-election that the Party's first MP was elected. Other Plaid Cymru candidates did well at by-elections in the industrial constituencies of Rhondda West and Caerphilly in 1967 and 1968 and, as in Scotland at the same time, the Party of nationalism came to be accepted as a respectable alternative to the older Parties. Two Plaid Cymru MPs were returned for Caernarvon and Merioneth in February 1974 and Gwynfor Evans re-won Carmarthen in October 1974. Thus there are now three Plaid Cymru MPs.

The growth of these movements reflects both the frustration with the failure of central government in London and a re-emergence of national identity. Plaid Cymru is deeply rooted in rural Wales, where the language is strong, but it would not be the rising force that it is unless concern for the language had been reinforced by concern about declining industries. It is in Scotland, however, that the Nationalists are strongest. As well as holding 11 of the 71 Scottish seats, the SNP are lying second in 42 seats—35 of them now held by Labour. The discovery of oil has only added to a general feeling of national pride and consciousness. The Kilbrandon Report on the constitution was established in part because of the Nationalist pressures. At present legislation is being prepared in the Cabinet Office which is likely to provide for a Scottish Assembly in Edinburgh. Any solution in which powers were granted to a Scottish Executive might well lead to the necessity of a written Constitution perhaps involving a referendum in the event of change.

The policy of the SNP at the last Election was that it would support moves for British withdrawal while continuing to demand Scottish representation in the organizations of the Common Market. The SNP thus opposes membership within the UK but proposes that when Scotland has its own government the Scottish people should decide the issue of their membership of the EEC through a referendum. Plaid Cymru also oppose the Common Market but the issue is seen as tangential to their main aspiration for political independence.

The holding of the Referendum on a regional and county basis will reveal whether Scottish and Welsh voters agree with the Nationalist line on Europe. A strongly differentiated vote against the Market might increase the pressures for self-government, pressures which it might be difficult to satisfy by the type of assembly at present envisaged. If at some future General Election the SNP gained a majority of Scottish seats in Parliament the demand for full self-government would be difficult to ignore. This would raise the question of whether a referendum should beheld on the issue and, if so, what would be the constituency? Would Scotland vote alone on independence or would the UK vote on its own dismemberment?

6 Public Opinion and the EEC

Throughout the period 1959-1967 opinion polls published in the Gallup Political Index showed pro-Market support running significantly ahead of anti-Market support. The question asked during the bulk of·the period was whether the respondants would approve or disapprove of the Government's deciding to join the European Common Market if the Government decided that by doing this the British interest would be best served. Especially during the first half of the 1960s, however, a high proportion of respondants replied 'Don't Know'.

The peak of approval for entry was in July 1966 when 71% were reported as being in favour if the Government felt entry was in Britain's best interests. This preceded the Labour Government's decision in the autumn of that year to investigate the terms of entry.

However, in May 1967, in a Gallup poll, only 36% answered affirmatively to the question 'Do you approve or disapprove of the Government applying for membership of the European Common Market?'. 41% disapproved of applying for membership in that month. Support had fallen but it was not until February 1970 that a new low for disapproval of membership was reached. In that month 57% disapproved and only 22% approved. As we mentioned in chapter 1 the low public support for membership in the period 1970–71 came as the Labour Party was moving towards a stance hostile to entry to the EEC on the Tory terms.

NOP and Gallup Poll show some increase in pro-Market support from July and late October 1971 respectively but those disapproving of Britain's joining the Common Market still exceeded those approving:

Date	Approve	Disapprove	Don't Know
March, 1972	40	43	17
October, 1972	38	46	16
January, 1973	44	41	15
June, 1973	37	49	13
October, 1973	34	51	15
February, 1974	36	52	12

Trends in Public Opinion: 1972–1974.*

The question in the above table was, for the period up to January 1973: 'Do you approve or disapprove of Britain's joining the Common Market?'. From January 1973 on the question was 'Do you approve or disapprove of Britain being a member of the Common Market?' This pattern was maintained till the more recent revival in Market support in 1975 in answer to questions specifically about voting intentions in the Referendum.

Finally it should be said that the press is both overwhelmingly pro-Market—only the *Morning Star* is against British membership—and hostile to the referendum. Rather than converting, however, the effect of the media has generally been that of crystallizing and re-enforcing opinion. In the referendum voters will not be able to fall back on their traditional Party allegiances and

---

* NOP Market Research Limited. Table appears as appendix to 'The Effect of Alternative wording on the outcome of the EEC Referendum' Report February, 1975.

this could lead either to apathy or to an increased susceptibility to change. Volatility has already been noted as a marked characteristic of the British electorate at recent General Elections. During the campaign periods there have been considerable swings in public support and opinion has also been sensitive to last-minute issues and dramas which have been played up by the press. It remains to be seen whether the present pro-Market majority (in the opinion polls) is subject to the same erosion or volatility in what could be a bitter last few weeks of the campaign.

In April 1975 in answer to the question: 'If the question in the Referendum were "Do you think that the UK should stay in the European Community (the Common Market)" how would you vote?' 57% replied 'YES, stay in', 28% 'NO, leave' and 15% 'don't know'. Among Conservative respondents the split was 68-23% and among Liberals 62-27%; Labour respondents showed a narrow majority 52-31% for staying in.*

Two further points concern the importance of the Government's recommendation that we stay in and the volatility of the British electorate on the Common Market issue. The Gallup Political Index of February 1975 (Report No. 175)** reported the results of a poll in which a sample were asked the following question:

If you could vote tomorrow on whether we should stay in the Common Market or leave it, how would you vote or wouldn't you vote at all?

33% replied that they would vote to stay in, while 41% would vote to leave and 12% would not vote (14% don't know). It is worth adding that a further poll showed that 50% felt that Britain was wrong to join the Common

---

* The poll conducted by Gallup Polls appeared in the *Daily Telegraph*. The interviewing period was from 17–21 April.
** Interviews 15–20 January, 1975.

Market. A third poll of the same date, however, gave rather different results:

> If the Government negotiated new terms for Britain's membership of the Common Market, and they thought it was in Britain's interests to remain a member, how would you vote then—to stay in or leave it?

Stay In	53%
Leave	22%
Wouldn't vote	6%
Don't know	19%

The Government's decision to recommend entry may thus be crucial. In addition a result favourable to continued membership (which at present looks likely) may hide a considerable antipathy towards the EEC. The negative arguments for continued membership may well be decisive. However, attitudes towards the Common Market have shown considerable volatility. The responsiveness of an NOP sample to differences in the wording of the question on the Common Market in February 1975 suggests a continued high degree of uncertainty about the issue.* One observer has suggested that this may increase the impact of the mass media on the referendum.**

Although a number of constituency parties and associations will remain neutral or be split and there will be little of the normal incentive to get the local vote out, other factors may contribute to a high poll. As we write opinion polls indicate high interest in the campaign. In a Gallup Poll of April 1975 in which respondents were asked how interested they were in the issue of whether Britain stayed in or left the Community, 39% were very interested, 35% moderately interested and 26% only a little interested. In addition there is likely to be a very

---

* NOP Market Research Limited. The Effect of Alternative Wording on the outcome of the EEC Referendum February, 1975.
** James Curran (1975).

high level of publicity, the issue will be clear and there may well be a feeling that on such a subject people 'ought' to vote.

At British post-war elections turn-out has varied between 72 and 84%. On Scandinavian experience a high poll might tend to favour a 'YES' vote. Thus Harold Wilson has in some ways a dilemma between on the one hand restraining the debate and conflict within his Party and on the other dramatizing the issue (and so provoking conflict in his Party) by using his office to make a strong appeal for approval of membership.

As 5 June approaches it is likely that the Prime Minister may be drawn increasingly into the campaign. Whatever the result it is difficult to see the Labour Party emerging without the losing wing feeling great bitterness. If the vote is 'NO' it remains to be seen whether Harold Wilson and James Callaghan, after 'successfully' renegotiating the terms, could lead the Party and the country out of Europe.

5 Implications of the Referendum

The prospect of a referendum poses a new situation for Parliament as well as for the country. Since at least the middle of the last century there have been continuous complaints that the House of Commons is out of date, ineffective and fails to represent the wishes of the people. The fact that these criticisms have gone on for so long and yet the House of Commons and even the House of Lords survive does not necessarily prove them wrong.

But until lately these criticisms have mainly taken the form of demanding a new party or a combination of existing parties. Before the first world war both Joseph Chamberlain and Lloyd George, among leading politicians, expressed dissatisfaction with the working of the party system. Between the wars there were several attempts to create new Parties. There have never been only two Parties in Parliament. In the past there were Canningites, Peelites, the Irish, the Fourth Party, the Labour Party and now the Liberal Party, the SNP, Plaid Cymru and the United Unionists exist as minority Parties. In fact, throughout the 19th century the forms of governments usually entailed bargaining between different groups. Palmerston, who was in major office for 40 years, always sat very lightly to Party discipline.

But the attempt to form a new Party between the two wars was based perhaps on more conscious dissatisfaction with the existing Parties than had existed in the 19th century. The first major attempt under Lloyd George was due no doubt to the personal position of the Prime Minister. He had no substantial Party of his own. He was

106

therefore compelled to look to his Tory friends for continuing support. But though, as with the Referendum itself, the suggestion of new political devices arose from the particular situation of the Government, it was also an attempt to meet what was felt to be a genuine defect in the Parliamentary system. After the collapse of Lloyd George's bid for continued power, we had the New Party. After that there was in the late 30s, not only the appearance of a Fascist Party, but a short-lived attempt to form a Popular Front.

During this period the alleged short-comings of the established Parties were largely connected with their inability to deal with the economic situation and their resistance to new thought. There was not so much emphasis on criticizing Parliament for being unrepresentative. Nevertheless, if one reads the biographies and debates of this period there was continuous discussion among MPs about their position in Parliament and their relationship with their constituents. There were continued attacks upon upon the 'old gangs' of both the Conservative and Labour Parties. These senior politicians were often accused of being hostile to new ideas, e.g. those of Maynard Keynes, which were alone felt to be capable of dealing with unemployment.

But so long as the supremacy of Parliament and the legitimacy of centralized government, to which we have already referred, were unchallenged, new devices such as the Referendum were not much canvassed. We have already referred to their support by Balfour and Baldwin but such support was temporary and designed to provide a way out of particular situations of difficulty for their parties. It is rather surprising that more has not been made of these precedents by the Labour Party. History sometimes seems to be repetitive.

The following assumptions were still accepted: first, that the MP rested upon a genuine democratic assent. It was given to him partly as an individual representing a constituency but also as a party member. The majority of the nation could still without too much unreality be divided, if not into two Parties, at least into two blocs or two coalitions. It was implicitly assumed that if someone said they were a Socialist you could from that deduce their general attitude across a whole range of political issues. The ideology of politics was important. It was also argued that Parties rested upon certain real social divisions. This meant that on the whole the bulk of the nation could feel that their views were at least made known and if they attracted any serious support would have some effect. The debating chamber of the House of Commons could be influenced by speeches and not numbers of Members or strength of votes.

Since the war the dissatisfaction with Parliament has taken rather new forms. There is wide dissatisfaction with the Party system as such and not merely with the existing Parties. The attempt to form new Parties in and just after the war again failed. But the failure was not only due to the strength of the existing Parties but to the fact that the hopes of those who might have supported them could probably not now be met by any Party on the established model. Fewer and fewer people came to think of their Party as expressing their opinions across the whole spectrum of politics. Not only on the Common Market but on defence and economic issues and indeed on the general role of Britain in the world the Parties were internally split. The controversy over nuclear armaments is a prime example of this situation. From time to time, particularly in the 60s, there was a move for a realignment of the Parties. Jo Grimond and some other Liberals made the suggestion that the natural division in politics was between the Conservatives and on the progressive side a broadly based national democratic Party embracing the Liberal Party and a considerable number of Labour supporters flanked by a completely socialist Party further left. Further, the Liberal Party was reduced to a very small number of Members though it retained a substantial vote in the country and other points of view were not represented in Parliament at all. Many people felt that they were not represented in the House of Commons. But, worse, they also felt that matters in which they believed passionately, including for instance, workers participation, were not even discussed.

If the indecisive 1974 elections are a sign of the shape of things to come, with both major Parties polling considerably less than their traditional electoral support then the two Party system as some have known it may be eroding. This is apart from the disruptive pressures within the Parties which may be encouraged by the Common Market campaign and the general emergence of other issues to which traditional Party ideology is not relevant. But the life left in the two major Parties should not be underestimated. As we have mentioned, in recent elections the two major Parties have paid more attention to their manifestos. Even the Conservatives have given more pledges at elections than has been their custom. Rather as the two American Parties have tried successfully to ensure that third Parties do not become too strong, so the British Parties will have every incentive to differentiate and alter their policies, in order to capture the support of the disaffected on new issues that emerge and thus maintain their dominance.

At the same time many people were frustrated by the failure of Britain, in spite of its immense technological power, to meet the expectations which were aroused by public authorities and by advertising. The feeling that our Government was not only undemocratic but incompetent grew stronger. As far as Members of Parliament were concerned, they found that they were becoming more and more involved in personal cases or in particular areas of

Parliamentary business. The general power of Parliament to control and criticize the Government was weakened. The debates upon the floor of the House of Commons were felt to be less and less significant. The election of a number of new Labour Members who made politics their whole time business and many of whom were in fact teachers of one sort or another, interested in positive participation in politics, increased this general tendency. They wanted to get into the business of government itself. They were not content that MPs should confine themselves largely to criticizing and to representing the dissatisfaction of their Parties or their constituencies. They had an appetite for blue books and white papers, for committees and for policy suggestions. All this tended to remove the business of Parliament from the floor of the House of Commons and to play down the great debates on over-riding issues. It is significant that the Parties which have captured votes from the three main traditional Parties are those associated with simple and clearly defined policy. The demands of the SNP and Plaid Cymru are simple—home rule. The demands of the Ulster Unionists are also in essence simple—union with Britain. But politics are now concerned with such an enormous range of issues, many of them managerial, that the Conservative, Labour or Liberal Parties find it impossible to make such a simple appeal which can at once rally all their members and identify them clearly in the public mind.

At the same time that Parliament and the main Parties have been losing their power and their appeal three other tendencies have appeared on the political scene. First, the power of the Prime Minister has in certain ways increased. We do not subscribe to the view of British politics as becoming 'Presidential' but if the reader will apply a simple test of trying to write down the members of the present Government, let alone the members of the last

110

Tory Government, he will we think discover that even if the Prime Minister and the senior Ministers have not greatly fallen in stature, other Ministers have lost a good deal, at least in public estimation. As we pointed out in an earlier chapter, there is perhaps some affinity between the thinking behind the Presidential form of government and such devices of direct democracy as the Referendum.

Secondly, there has been a great increase in the power of extra parliamentary bodies. The Trades Unions are the most obvious but by no means the only ones. This is not a new situation. Indeed, was the general interest not constantly threatened by the self-interested pressures of various organizations, there would be little or no need for a government at all, except to keep the minimum of order. These bodies tend to go direct to the Government by-passing the representative system.

The third tendency has been the attempt at direct democracy sometimes described as 'community politics'. Often this has been no more than a determination to raise grievances or to press for such things as adventure playgrounds. But behind it there is in our estimation some wider feeling that the people want more say in government. There is also the feeling that the social services should take on a more communal attitude designed to prevent bad conditions arising in the poorer communities and not simply concerning themselves with individual cases of hardship due to these conditions.

Some of the points made above were noted both in the report of the Royal Commission on the Constitution itself and also in the Memorandum of Dissent. The latter, for instance, declared:

There has been a decline this century in the extent to which we as people govern ourselves.

again

The development of the main political parties and the

111

attendant Party discipline have also weakened the House of Commons as a check on the executive. The House as a whole no longer has an effective share in policy making that was the norm in the latter half of the 19th century.

or, particularly and most definitely:

The fact has to be faced that if we really believe that democracy means that people and their representatives should have a real share in political power, our institutions do not make adequate provision for this today.

It may well be noted in passing that the Kilbrandon Commission did not mention referenda. It is against this background that the referendum is taking place.

The holding of the referendum is itself an issue at this moment. On the whole, those who favour the Common Market are against the Referendum and vice versa. The division is by no means complete, however, and as we have said earlier some pro-Marketeers are not wholly unsympathetic to the Referendum.

The case for the Referendum rests on three legs. The first is simply that this is a unique issue. There is clearly a considerable amount of truth in this. The cases of the act of union between England and Scotland and the abolition of Grattan's Parliament were no doubt similar but they took place at quite different points in our Parliamentary development and they did not so directly affect England and Wales. The second argument is that the Referendum is one of a class of issues which can legitimately be called constitutional. As we have no written constitution, when the British use the word 'constitutional' we usually imply certain general customs in the conduct of politics. For instance, the 'checks and balances' are sometimes said to be constitutional. It is inevitably the case that the most successful British statesmen have felt that Britain was not governed either as a populist democracy nor by a simple majority in Parliament pressing through its own policies. The government of Britain had to be viewed as an organic matter, taking note of the past, looking to the future and having some respect for the views and rights of the minorities. The ultimate protection against extremist measures forced through against the continuing wishes of the electorate was the right of every Parliament to reverse the Acts of its predecessor. But though in some senses this could be done even on the issue of the Common Market, for in fact this Referendum itself is about taking Britain out of the Common Market and not to decide whether she goes in, yet the longer she remains in the Market, the more difficult would it be to reverse the act of accession. This can therefore be said to be a class of issue in which the normal constitutional safeguard of the people reversing the Acts of Government by expressing their will at a subsequent General Election is inoperative. This argument of course can also be used were the issue of Scottish independence to become dominant. As we have said earlier, already it has been accepted that referenda are a suitable method of deciding whether Northern Ireland shall join with Southern Ireland. This too, it could be argued, would be a state very difficult, if not impossible, to reverse. The third argument for the Referendum is simply that deduced from the account of our politics given above. Although it was a method explicitly rejected by Mr Wilson sometime ago, yet it has been generally assumed by most politicians that the failure to offer those who are against remaining in Europe a fair opportunity to express their views is an unsatisfactory situation. Mr Heath is constantly reminded that he said our entry into Europe must have the whole-hearted asent of the British people.

Those who argue against the Referendum also have a number of legs to their argument. They contend that a referendum undermines the authority of representative government. Some would rest their case on the very strong possibility that referenda will now be demanded on such matters as the future of Scotland and even possibly on the future of various other parts of the United Kingdom. (The counties of Orkney and Shetland who for most of their history have formed part of Scandinavia are toying with the idea of seceding from Scotland if it achieves home rule—carrying much of the oil with them.) Any such moves would no doubt lead to a demand for further referenda. But there are people who believe that once having accepted the referendum for any issue it will be difficult to confine it to those so-called 'constitutional' situations. In an earlier chapter we drew attention to the fact that in some countries which use the Referendum it has proved most effective on what are called 'Home Office' issues. Hanging is pre-eminently one of these issues. It is at least highly possible that were there a referendum on the re-introduction of hanging the 'ayes' would have it. Against this it must be remembered that the progressives won the referendum on divorce in Italy. Nevertheless, the possibility of the referendum spreading to 'Home Office' issues causes considerable alarm among its opponents. There is then the argument that if we are afraid that Parliament will lose sovereignty if we join Europe, how much greater is the loss of sovereignty through a referendum? For we have seen that a Referendum must be an attempt to go over the heads of the elected representatives. No longer can the Burkian thesis be applied even in theory if the referendum is to be mandatory. There is then the point that very difficult situations could obviously arise if the views of Parliament differ from the majority in a referendum. So long as the Referendum is merely advisory the difficulty would not be acute. But a referendum which forces a Government either to resign or act against its better judgement would fundamentally alter the whole British system. In the present situation the Government have said that they still consider themselves bound by the Referendum. This in itself is somewhat peculiar. Many would think it a strange situation that a Government, two-thirds of whose members feel strongly that ruin stares them in the face if we come out of Europe, could remain in office to do just that. It was indeed the holding of the Referendum which originally led Mr Jenkins and others to leave the Shadow Cabinet. Equally, it will be strange if the other one-third who have been preaching doom if we remain in Europe can stay in office. It may well be that, if the people reject the advice of the Government that they should remain in Europe, Mr Wilson will have to resign, whatever he may say to the contrary. It is difficult to believe that anyone else could form a Government from the Labour Party. It is even harder to believe that the Conservatives, the great bulk of whom are now in favour of staying in Europe, could form a government or indeed would be asked to do so. The likely outcome would be that Mr Wilson would be granted a dissolution. It is not our business in this book to go too far into the realms of speculation. But we don't think it is pre-judging the issue to say that it is hard to see how a General Election would solve the matter given an anti EEC vote. The fact would remain that the Conservative and Labour Parties and two-thirds of the Cabinet would have committed themselves up to the hilt during the campaign for the Referendum that the future of this country demanded that we should remain in the Common Market. And most people are agreed that accession to the EEC is no minor matter. We cannot see, therefore, any good prospects for an effective government after a General Election still presumably governed by Mr Wilson's doctrine that is mandated to taking us out of Europe.

However, of course, the most important issues of the campaign are the arguments for and against remaining in Europe itself. These we have mentioned in a previous chapter. There are very many issues concerned with

Europe but some are emerging more strongly.

There is the argument over sovereignty. Those who wish to remain in maintain that Britain has already surrendered sovereignty both de jure to international institutions, e.g. NATO, and de facto owing to her declining power in the world. They argue that the 19th century concept of the wholly self-contained national state is in any case out of date. They believe that sovereignty is not a theoretical matter but a practical question of power. Britain, according to them, can exert more power and influence in the world from within the European community than outside it. As against this, those who wish to come out point out that the surrender of sovereignty to international institutions such as NATO is in their view of a different order from that entailed in joining a new political organization such as Europe. Although it may be that monetory union and a federal Europe are now in cold storage, nevertheless, already many decisions previously within the exclusive power of the British Parliament will be taken in Brussels. There is the residual veto but opponents of remaining in the EEC feel it is insufficient. Further, if the EEC is a success demand for a more democratically elected European Parliament with more power will grow. If the EEC is a failure, we shall find ourselves hampered from taking the necessary independent action by quarrels within the EEC.

The line of argument over sovereignty is coming into particular prominence owing to the economic situation. On the one hand it is argued that if Britain remains on her own her economy is so weak that she can exert no influence. On the other hand, it is said that if we deny ourselves the right to impose tariffs against our partners in the Six our industry could not withstand the flood of imports which threaten us.

There is a division between those who think that the British economy can only survive within the larger market

116

provided by Europe and those tho think that we should be flooded by the more efficient European industries.

The arguments on prices appear to be somewhat less important than they were a few months ago. According to the Government's white paper the effect of prices on having joined the Community has been small. Though many people still blame our membership of the Community for high prices, many more, however, see them as due partly to world conditions and partly to the inflationary situation in this country itself. On the other hand, those who favour staying in the EEC put increasing weight on the disastrous effect they foretell upon the pound if we withdraw.

The CAP is probably not as provocative a cause of contention as it was. The NFU have come out in favour of remaining in Europe. It has been realized that British farmers have gained to some extent by getting cheaper feeding stuffs within the community than they could have got outside it. The invervention price system, though not universally popular, is gaining some acceptance and it is realized that the access to a large European agricultural market has its advantages. Nevertheless, there remains a strong feeling that the CAP ought to be amended and that the British system of guaranteed prices was a good one. The stories of butter mountains are firmly embedded in the national memory.

One of the most powerful arguments for the existence of the EEC was that it would remove the possibilities of wars in Western Europe and particularly between France and Germany. When we look at the last thousand years of European history this indeed was a worthy objective. It has been said too that the EEC is essential for the under-pinning of NATO. In its turn, NATO has proved an effective deterrent against Russian aggression. These probably remain powerful arguments with the older generation and among those intimately connected with foreign affairs. It is doubtful if they are felt to be so important by others. Perhaps simply because the Rhine is no longer a potential theatre of war it is coming to be argued that in any case further wars in Western Europe are extremely unlikely, Common Market or not.

The whole argument over defence in Britain is now at a low ebb, no doubt consequent upon her greatly diminished role in foreign affairs. Some people feel that the danger of being closely linked with countries some of whom have an unstable history and two at least large Communist minorities outweigh any advantages in the field of external defence.

Many MPs may feel the pressures in the campaign most directly when they meet particular industries or groups among their constituents. Fishermen, for instance, are frightened that free access will be given to boats from the EEC right up to the coast of Britain. The situation over fishing is quite instructive when we look at the general pattern and pressures of the campaign. It so happens that the Referendum is coinciding with a severe loss of confidence in the fishing industry. This loss of confidence is partly due to the effects of inflation. There has been a recession in some parts of the market, particularly in America. The fishing industry has become very much aware of the gross over-fishing of the North Sea. 'Industrial' fishing for very small fish, prout, sand eels, etc. not for human consumption but for animal feeding stuffs or fertilizers is also causing great alarm. The bulk of this over-fishing is at present caused by countries outside the EEC, particularly Norway, the Eastern European countries and, to a smaller extent, Faroe and Iceland. Pro Common Market fishermen have pointed out that the great market for herring is within the EEC. The EEC provide grants for fishing boats. It is said that the whole question of limits must be reconsidered in the light of the findings of the conference on the law of the sea.

118

After this re-consideration steps will have to be taken to protect stocks. We quote fishing merely as an example of how comparatively local issues may operate.

The pro-Marketeers are fond of asking what is the alternative to staying in? They inquire where else we could find a free market for our goods comparable to Europe, which is the largest free market in the world. If the anti-Marketeers respond with some resurrection of EFTA, the pro-Marketeers point out that membership of EFTA involved a substantial diminution of sovereignty and interference with our control over our own industrial development. They cite, for instance, the objection by the Norwegians to the British government's subsidy towards aluminium smelters. If the anti-Marketeers point out that Norway and other countries have concluded satisfactory trading arrangements with the EEC, the answer comes back that Norway supplies goods which are needed by the EEC industries and do not compete. They further claim that a small country like Norway is in a very different situation from large, highly industrialized Britain and that in all such arrangements the EEC lays down strict rules.

The Commonwealth now favours Britain's entry. The Lomé agreement has done much to allay the fears of those who saw the EEC as a rich man's club inimical to the underdeveloped countries.

There is the pressure of inertia. It takes an effort now to come out. MPs such as Sir Derek Walker-Smith who was against entry now favour remaining in, being influenced by the breach of our Treaty obligations which withdrawal might be said to entail.

None of these disputes will probably influence many ordinary voters though the fading of the prophecies of doom which were made about Norway if she refused accession will no doubt have some weight particularly in Scotland.

In Scotland, and in Wales too, the European issue is intertwined in some people's mind with the Home Rule issue. To the SNP it is intolerable that Scotland should be carried into the EEC by England. They stress the superior economic position which they maintain Scotland now occupies owing to the oil discoveries. They can argue therefore that the dangers to the British economy and the British pound which might flow from withdrawal do not apply to Scotland. But against this can be urged Scotland's long association with the Continent and the more continental tradition of her law and universities.

In Northern Ireland all the major Parties are in favour of withdrawing from the Market. They support the Referendum but the United Ulster unionists are anxious that its form should give no credence to the view that Northern Ireland is not a part of the UK.

The more idealistic motives which were strong some years back are still urged, especially by some Liberals, as a reason for retaining membership, but now they seem weaker. So does the fear of the Left that membership of the Common Market will put a brake on further socialist measures. It was noticeable, however, that the Foreign Secretary summing up the debate on the Government's White Paper stressed that we were, and intended to remain, a mixed economy. Our economy has already benefited to the tune of some £290 million from EEC grants but neither this on the one side not the failure to find a satisfactory attitude to the OPEC countries on the other seems likely to bulk large in the public mind.

The points which emerge from this are that votes on the Referendum will no doubt be influenced by the particular situation of many of the voters. If their industry is depressed they may be inclined to vote against remaining in Europe, partly as a protest against Government policy and partly because Europe may be in their eyes a scapegoat for their troubles. It is indeed difficult to

120

disentangle the effects of being in the EEC from the general effects of the situation in the world at large. The Referendum will not be decided upon a calm consideration confined to the known results of joining the EEC.

For instance, in a different area, those who want to come out of the EEC have laid great stress upon our adverse balance with our colleague countries. But pro-Marketeers point out that in any case we would have to have bought the goods which have caused this imbalance from somewhere. The price would certainly have been as high if not higher than in Europe and, further, the adverse balance is due to the need to buy the goods and not to the fact that we are in Europe.

We are conscious that the vote may well be influenced also by the economic situation of Britain as a whole. The Government have claimed that on one important matter, our contribution to the European budget, they have got considerable concessions. But what no one is able to tell with certainty is how far these concessions would have been obtained anyway from the natural evolution of the EEC, nor indeed, what they may mean in years to come.

A further factor is that there may be an anti-EEC vote aimed as a protest against the Government. Indeed it may be a protest against all the main parties. The Referendum could give the public an opportunity to clobber the Establishment for reasons quite divorced from Europe.

It would seem to us that the pro-EEC campaign may be conducted at too high a speculative and general level to reassure the fears of the minority groups. However, the minority groups remain minorities. No doubt the bulk of the population will vote on a vaguer feeling that somehow or other the future will be better or worse off according as to whether we stay in or leave Europe. It would appear at present from the opinion polls that most people feel we should stay in. In the end it may well be a political hunch rather than nice but problematical economic judgements which will determine the public's vote. And the public may well be right in judging this as a political decision.

The opinion polls are now a striking feature of our political life. It could be argued that the Referendum is more acceptable than it might have been 10 or 20 years ago because people have got used to these polls. Indeed it could perhaps be added to the list of arguments in favour of a referendum that if we are to have opinion polls we might as well have properly conducted tests of national opinion. How far polls actually affect the result is not a matter with which this book is concerned. But it would be wrong to leave out an account of the effect of polls on the public mind during the Referendum. If they are powerful during Elections, as some people think, they may be even more powerful during a referendum. In an Election people are still to some extent influenced by the local campaign and the personality of the candidate. They can also discount opinion polls as not being representative of their area or its likely result. But during a referendum the opinion poll is being carried out on exactly the same ground as the ultimate result. Further, the phrasing of the question and the general presentation of the matter at issue follow rather closely the customs of the polsters. One such polster has offered his advice on how the Referendum should be phrased.

Editorially the national press is overwhelmingly in favour of remaining in the Common Market. The opposite view probably has a relatively strong following among journalists. The anti-Marketeers get a fair share of news coverage. Indeed remembering the penchant of our newspapers for sensation and perhaps for the side which can create most trouble it may well be that the anti-Marketeers, represented rightly or wrongly as the challenging Party, may come off best. Sweet reason on either side may be discounted.

122

Since this is our first experience of a campaign of this kind it is difficult to tell how the media or the public will respond. Will public interest be fanned to a high pitch in the concluding stages of the Referendum—if for no other reason then simply because it will be seen as a stimulating horse-race? Or will those who shrug their shoulders and say it is all too difficult grow in numbers?

The campaign is being carried out both by the official organizations of the main Parties and by unofficial Party organizations where there is substantial dissent from the Party line. There are also two 'umbrella' organizations which have certain features unique in British history. There have been great movements outside the Parties, e.g. the anti-Corn Law League and the Chartists. These have included members of more than one Party. There was the attempt to form a 'Popular Front' before the war. But never before have there been two quasi-official organizations cutting clean across Party lines but with government finance and official recognition on the BBC etc. The spectacle of the reigning Home Secretary campaigning against some of his colleagues in Government as President of the 'Britain in Europe' campaign with the last Tory Prime Minister, the latest General Secretary of the TUC, a member of the Opposition Front Bench, the ex-leader of the Liberal Party, the President of the NFU and a prominent retired member of the Foreign Office as Vice Presidents is an entirely new development. It could have all sorts of repercussions which cannot be pursued in this book. Every kind of British custom is broken. Cabinet responsibility, party solidarity, provision of public funds for partisan purposes, and even the involvement of active or only just retired officials in such a controversy are new developments. The issue has served also to emphasize the cohesion of the Tribune group as a block active within the Labour Party.

No particular political developments are ever isolated from the general trend of politics. Mounting inflation and the apparent loss of power by successive governments, the demand for new political initiatives and even for a coalition will have their effect not only upon the campaign but upon the aftermath. There is already much criticism of the reform of local government which has been accompanied by a great increase in the number of officials and the rise in the rates. To some people more government and more bureaucrats in Brussels added to the prospect of Scottish and Welsh Assemblies appears alarming.

The Government's view is apparently that once the Referendum is over, the Common Market dispute will die and politics will return to their old mould. We have some doubts about this. It is difficult, as we have said, to see how the Government can ever be quite the same. But will not the 'umbrella' organization forge alignments difficult to break? Alignments for which there is already some latent demand?

Will this national vote be a further step towards presidential government? Or may it emphasize the centrifugal forces at work in the United Kingdom? Since the difficulties of electors torn between the desire to support their Parties but dissenting on this issue could have been met, at least to some extent by Proportional Representation, will the Referendum give rise to new interest in electoral reform? Already the presence of six Parties in Parliament and the supposed threat of domination by extreme minorities have assumed new interest in changes in the voting system. Other political expedients may be canvassed. The Referendum is not only a unique event in itself but it has swept aside the block which in the minds of most people has prevented drastic changes in our representative government. The debates in the House of Commons committee have released new thoughts about the relationship of the Member to his constituents. The mere fact that a national count was rejected on a free vote is significant. Many Labour Members have claimed that they will consider themselves bound by the national result. The count by counties and regions is in itself a new departure. On the one hand it may release members from direct constituency pressures, particularly important for pro-Market Labour MPs. On the other hand it is a rejection of the plebiscitary aspect of a national vote ignoring local difficulties. Many MPs still maintain that they would like to know how their constituents vote even if they disagree. The count by regions and counties may emphasize not only the different views of Scotland, Wales and England, but perhaps different regional views within England—giving a fillip to demands for further devolution. It is difficult to see how the Referendum can fail to have important long-term repercussions. At first sight it is a further blow at the representative system, already losing influence. It is just possible, however, that by releasing a general debate about the political system as a whole it might lead to reforms which will actually increase the power of the MP. Indeed it is difficult to believe that our association with Europe, whether it is maintained or rejected, can be taken out of political controversy by one vote (which may be narrow and on a small poll) in a single referendum.

So this political expedient, reached by such a curious route, could well end by realigning the parties, transforming the representative system and forcing the reform of our parliamentary procedures without deciding the European debate. The political forces released by the Referendum are unlikely to be put back in the bottle this June.

Sources and Bibliography

The sources given are by no means exhaustive. A number of works of related interest to each chapter are cited.

Chapter 1
The main sources are the *Times* and *Guardian*, Labour Party Conference Reports and Official documents. Other sources include:

Uwe Kitzinger, *Diplomacy and Persuasion* (1973)

Robert J. Lieber, *British Politics and European Unity* (1970)

James Bellini, *British entry: Labour's Nemesis. Young Fabian pamphlet No. 30* (May 1972)

Harold Wilson, *The Labour Government. A Personal Record* (1971)

George Brown, *In My Way* (1972)

Section 4 draws heavily on Kitzinger (1973) and on 'How Wilson took the lonely road back from Europe', *Sunday Times*, July 18th, 1971.

Chapter 2

A. H. Birch, *Representative and Responsible Government*. (1964).

R. Benewick and T. Smith (eds.), *Direct Action and Democratic Politics*.

R. T. McKenzie, *British Political. Parties*. (2nd ed. 1963).

S. H. Beer, *Modern British Politics*.

A. Benn, *A Socialist Reconaissance*. Fabian Society. (November 1970).

127

Chapter 3

C. Hughes. *Switzerland* (1975).

Ingunn Norderral Means. 'Norway and the EEC', *Scandinavian Studies* Vol. 46 No. 4. (Fall 1974).

Henry Valen. 'Norway "NO" to EEC', *Scandinavian Political Studies* Vol. 8. (1973).

O. Hellerik and N. P. Gleditsch. 'The Common Market decision in Norway', *Scandinavian Political Studies*. Vol. 8 (1973).

Colin Braham, J. Burton. *The Referendum Reconsidered*. Fabian Tract 434 (March, 1975).

Philip C. Goodhart. *Referendum* (1971).

C. Sharp. 'The Case Against the Referendum'. Fabian Tract 155 (1911).

Chapters 4 and 5

Plaid Cymru Research Group. *Wales and the Common Market*, Referendum Study Papers (April, 1975).

James Curran. *The Role of the Mass Media in the Common Market Referendum*. (mimeo) (March, 1975).

Barry Hedges and Roger Jowell. *Britain and the EEC*. Social and Community Planning Research (July, 1971).

NOP Market Research Limited. *The Effect of Alternative Wording on the Outcome of the EEC Referendum* (February, 1975).

Roger Jowell and James Spence. *The Grudging Europeans*. A Study of British Attitudes towards the EEC (March, 1975).

Referendum on United Kingdom Membership and the European Community. February, 1975. Cmmd. 5925.

Membership of the European Community Report on Renegotiations. March, 1975. Cmmd. 6003.